# The Forgotten American

(Shattered Dreams)

by

Paula B. Compton

The contents of this work, including, but not limited to, the accuracy of events, people, and places depicted; opinions expressed; permission to use previously published materials included; and any advice given or actions advocated are solely the responsibility of the author, who assumes all liability for said work and indemnifies the publisher against any claims stemming from publication of the work.

All Rights Reserved
Copyright © 2015 by Paula B. Compton

No part of this book may be reproduced or transmitted, downloaded, distributed, reverse engineered, or stored in or introduced into any information storage and retrieval system, in any form or by any means, including photocopying and recording, whether electronic or mechanical, now known or hereinafter invented without permission in writing from the publisher.

Dorrance Publishing Co
585 Alpha Drive
Suite 103
Pittsburgh, PA 15232
Visit our website at *www.dorrancebookstore.com*

ISBN: 978-1-4809-1829-0
eISBN: 978-1-4809-1806-1

To Kandace, my precious daughter, who brought me more joy than I could have ever imagined. She encouraged me to write this story so other survivors of discrimination, abuse, and domestic violence might understand there is a better tomorrow.

The story was inspired by true events, but the names have been changed.

# Acknowledgments

Three people provided valuable assistance to the final product. First, I would like to thank Sandy Cogen for proofreading the initial draft. Second, I would like to thank Jennifer A. Gregory, author and writing consultant at *gejanovels.com,* who critiqued and edited the final draft. Third, I would like to thank the firm of Starvin' Artist Graphic Design for designing the book cover.

# Contents

The Pain of Adultery and Divorce: Chapters 1 – 23 . . . . . . . . . . . . . . . . . . . . . . 1
Starting a New Life: Chapters 24 – 38 . . . . . . . . . . . . . . . . . . . . . . . . . . . . 89
Work Abroad and Private Sector: Chapters 39 – 49 . . . . . . . . . . . . . . . . . . . 143

## Chapter 1

I married a young man by the name of Lester in April 1966. I remember those words so vividly: "To have and to hold, from this day forward, for better, for worse, for richer, for poorer, in sickness or in health, to love and to cherish 'til death do us part. And hereto I pledge you my faithfulness." I took the vows seriously and believed I would be married for life. I loved him. We would have children, raise them, and grow old, then die. It was as simple as that.

Lester graduated from college the year before and worked for a federal agency in New Mexico. The year we met, I already had two and a half years of college behind me and worked full time. Then marriage came along. I was a wife now. Returning to college for my junior year didn't fit with the image of a homemaker, despite my independence. I went to college to become an archeologist so I could collect information on past human cultures. I dreamed about going on excavations in foreign countries.

In New Mexico, change came slowly; like the shimmer of dry heat crawling up some dirt road to nowhere. As kids, we might have complained, thought our lot in life was unfair, looked at our parents, their faces tired, hot, and thought we could do better. I knew I could. Yet for most, it was easiest to be the same. Default to homemaker, shirtdress, and white picket fence. Perhaps for some, the heat makes you do the same things; it is easier that way, demands less energy. Well, it lit a fire under my feet, made me want to do something. I was serious. People all through school knew it. I could have both a career and a family. Most thought me nuts and an oddball.

Many Europeans refer to Native Americans as "the forgotten Americans" or "the real Americans." As a Native American (the forgotten American) who lived in an all-white neighborhood and always the only brown-skinned individual in most settings in the early stages of my life, I had become rather reserved. Back in the 1950s and 1960s, many people in the western states still had a stereotypical perception of all Native Americans as "merciless Indian savages." I made sure I was never boisterous or obnoxious for fear people would think I was "an Indian savage." And so I became anonymous, made it easier that way, could feel unseen in a world from where there was no hiding.

This description of Native American as "merciless Indian savages" is in the United States Declaration of Independence, signed by the original thirteen states on July 4, 1776. The Declaration states, "All men are created equal and have certain unalienable rights such as life, liberty, and the pursuit of happiness." But this did not include the original inhabitants. Denied citizenship until 1924, the sad history of Native Americans has long been marginalized at best, but more often ignored in the United States. However, our foreign friends and foes abroad know the history of the Native Americans too well and are too happy to remind us of that sad history.

My father, who served in the United States Navy in World War II, experienced racism. Everyone in the Navy was required to work as a team, yet even the unifying nature of war did not prevent racist comments. "Dirty savage" or "red Injun" were not out of place among the white men my father served with. Yet he loved his country. To the end, he always reminded me to "be the best citizen you can be in this great land."

For my father, education meant a chance to rise above racism. A means with which to rise above the harmful stereotypes thrust upon us. To this end, in addition to understanding my own Native American culture, my father encouraged my education. He wanted me to succeed. In many ways, he was the fire beneath my feet. So racism and the Native-American experience set the stage for my life's journey. Yet even as "the forgotten American,", from the ashes of challenges and disappointment, I always rose to meet life's many rewards. The key is to never give up.

So there I was, young, married, excited, the world before me. Prior to permitting the man I loved to slip the ring on my finger, I had applied and was to attend summer school at the University of New Mexico in Albuquerque, where Lester was employed as a budget analyst. After getting married, I went to summer school as planned, but in the fall of that year, I discovered I was pregnant. Nine months later, my beautiful daughter Casey was born.

With thick brown hair and fair skin, one of the nurses thought Casey's father might be from the Dakotas, since many Native Americans from those parts were of mixed blood. Intermarriage with early French and English settlers had seen to that.

We loved and adored our new baby girl, who gave us so much joy through the years. Her father adored her and she quickly became "Daddy's girl." I remember when she was only six months old; he wanted to take her for a ride in the car. I objected at first but finally agreed. He strapped her into the baby carrier and drove her around the neighborhood, singing the latest popular songs to her.

## The Forgotten American

Lester knew I was interested in working to help with household expense. Shortly after having Casey, Lester came home one evening and said there was a position open in one of the offices within the federal agency where he was employed.

It was a clerical position that required typing billing vouchers for the federal government. I submitted my resume for the job and was pleased to be selected for the position in the early part of the summer months. We were able to find a wonderful older woman to take care of Casey five days a week. She was a kind and magnificent woman who also had several lovely grandchildren. She took excellent care of our Casey and treated her like one of her own grandchildren. I worked all that summer but made sure that I made time to play and take care of Casey in the evenings and on weekends.

## Chapter 2

From the day that Casey was born, I looked forward to giving her a positive and comfortable life. I was determined to provide her with the things I did not have while growing up. I wanted her to have a mother and father who not only loved her but also had the financial means to provide luxuries that I had only dreamed of during my childhood. I wanted her to have brand-name clothes; a car to drive to school when she was old enough to drive; and a huge, luxuriously furnished home. I wanted her to learn to play the piano, take ballet lessons, and learn to ski, play tennis, and other sports that were of interest to her. Little did I know that one day in the near future, my dreams and desires would be shattered in the blink of an eye.

I had big dreams for Casey, and in order to realize these dreams, I knew I had to go back to college soon. At fourteen, I was raising myself, working as a nanny for several neighborhood families, while attending school full time. All of this fell against the wishes of my father, who worried I might lose my education; however, it was my only way out of the Christian boarding school I hated with a passion. I was determined to succeed and rarely went out. While other girls attended social events and functions, I babysat, tutored and, on weekends, cleaned their houses. Cleaning houses was good. It opened me to a world of luxuries. While cleaning a master bedroom, I would dream of my own silk sheets one day, of having my own backyard pool, of sending my own child to tennis lessons, and of having my own live-in housekeeper.

Known for blending Christian principles with excellent academic training, my parents enrolled me in a Christian boarding school. The years I spent at this school were not happy ones. As I remember, from the day I entered that school to my last day on campus, the boys were always picking on me. They would stand in the hallway at recess time or after school and run toward me when I came out. They would begin to hit me in my arm or back but never in the face. I guess they knew a hit in the face would be very visible. The boys would also make fun of me every day and call me a "ram." I had very thick hair that was cut in a blunt-style fashion, so the ends of my hair close to my face would curl up like the horns of a ram. At first I did not know why they hit me or called me names, but later I learned it was because the teachers considered me to be a very bright child. I rarely received less than an A on my tests and homework. So to hurt me for being academically smart, they tormented me with their fists and name-calling.

When I arrived on campus, I had long thick braids that stretched to my waist. Within less than a day, the dormitory mother chopped off my long beautiful braids at chin length. The dormitory mother made sure we all got our hair cut in that fashion when we entered the school. This was part of the education process, which was still being used as the primary acculturation process for Native Americans and other minorities in the 1950s. Every student was forced to speak English, study standard subjects, attend church, and leave Native-American traditions and languages behind. When the school accepted us, our parents were never informed that our hair would be cut, which is not only wrong but also abusive by the school's authority. If someone did that today to my child without my permission, my lawyer and I would be meeting with the head of the school within a day.

When I entered the seventh grade, I could no longer stand the hateful boys and girls who made my life miserable. I also could no longer stand the teachers and others of authority who closed their eyes to the bullying that went on in that school. Bullying is considered to be new in our current school system, but as far as I am concerned, it always existed in certain segments of our school system. Back in the days when I was attending the Christian boarding school, it was not possible to tell anyone with authority about the physical and emotional bullying imposed on us. We would be told: "Now don't be a tattle tale," or "You should learn to get along with others," or "Mind your own business."

I have never forgotten one dormitory mother who supervised the junior high school girls. I did not know this woman but noticed that she never smiled at anyone. I was still living in the dormitory for elementary school girls but knew who she was because of her stone-like expression. One evening, I left the student dining room rather late because I had a second serving of dessert. There were only two or three students still eating at their table when I went into the dining room hallway, where everyone hung their coats.

I was searching for my coat when I heard a voice that said, "What are you still doing here?" I turned around and saw that it was the lady who never smiled. I said I was looking for my coat, and about that time, she had approached me from my right side. I looked up and, like many children I licked my lips. The next thing I heard was, "Don't you stick your tongue out at me." As she spoke, she slapped me across the face. I said ever so very quietly that I was not sticking my tongue out at her. She turned a deaf ear and slapped me again while stating that I was not to "sass her." I was so stunned that I could not even cry. I found my coat just as she turned to walk away.

I scurried really quickly back to my dorm but did not dare tell anyone what happened. I was embarrassed, ashamed, sad, and my heart ached like it was going to break in half. I could not even tell my parents because they believed in the teachings and discipline of the school faculty. When anything bad happened to me, whether it was my fault of not, I would always think of my father's frequent reminder: "If you are caught doing anything wrong, I will support the person with authority and not you."

I respected my parents, especially my dad for his teachings and strict disciplines. His physical, technical, and psychological training in the military were often used as examples of good basic teachings. I never talked back to my parents or said anything bad about them like many young people do today. I learned early in my childhood to understand and respect them because I knew they loved me.

## Chapter 3

In the fall of our second year of marriage, Lester was selected for a management internship with one of the federal agencies in Washington, D.C. He was scheduled to start the internship by the first of January, so we both resigned from our jobs in early December to prepare for our move to the East Coast. It did not take long to pack our household items since we were renting a fully furnished apartment. On the day of our cross-country move, the movers were able to load our household items into the huge moving van within less than one hour since we did not have many belongings.

On the way to Washington, D.C., we stopped to visit Lester's mother in South Dakota. After spending several days of visiting with relatives, we decided it was time to leave for our final destination. It was already Thursday and Lester was due to begin his new position that Monday morning. The weather was treacherous, blizzard conditions and lethal amounts of ice glazing the roads. Clearly, this was not a time to travel with a baby and looking back, I grow cold at the thought that we did it at all. But when you are young, I guess you do crazy things like that. In any case, we slid into D.C. on Friday evening, exhausted, road weary, and thanking God all the way.

The apartment reserved for us was a small, efficient place, with one bedroom, a living room, a kitchenette, and a laundry room. For one month we could stay at the expense of the federal agency while searching for a place of our own. Two weeks later, we discovered a small clean furnished apartment in Suitland, Maryland. A twenty-minute drive to D.C. back in the sixties, you could tack on about another sixty today.

I stayed home with Casey for a couple of months and then went to work at the same agency where Lester was working as an intern. Since I had not completed my college education, the only type of job I could find in the Washington Metropolitan area was in the clerical field. Lester's salary as an intern did not cover all of our expenses, so it was necessary for me to go to work shortly after we settled in Maryland. I applied for a clerk typist position that Lester said was being advertised where he worked. Within one week after applying for the position, I was selected.

Around this time, I began to notice changes in Lester's behavior I had not seen before. While I was at home caring for Casey, he would push me aside whenever he got angry. At the time, I thought he was tired, never realizing there might be anything more sinister than that.

The clerk typist position was in the office that managed the Job Corps program located on Native-American reservations. My job was to assist the secretary of the office with typing letters to the various Job Corps offices. The letters were standard letters and were fairly easy to type. It was an easy job, but I was not the best typist, and the secretary often caught typing errors. The first month I spent many hours retyping these letters, but eventually I became a pretty good typist. The one semester of typing class that I took in my senior year in high school was not enough to compete with girls coming out of secretarial schools. Because I never wanted to fail or be defeated in anything, I worked on my typing skills every day during my lunch hour. Gulping my lunch down was not good, but I did improve my typing skills very quickly.

We were fortunate to find a wonderful older woman called Big Mama to care for Casey. She had a small daycare center in her home. Big Mama lived about five minutes from us, and it was on the way to work, so everything worked out well for everyone. The daycare center had only five children, so I knew my daughter would be taken care of very well.

With little money to spend, we did not entertain nor did we go out to eat or for entertainment that cost more than the price of a drive-in movie on Saturdays. Cheap and popular with the young, you could have a great night out without breaking the bank in the 1960s. Going to church every Sunday was very important to Lester, who was raised as a Catholic.

Sunday was truly a day of rest for us. After church, we lounged about the small living room, watching old movies on the black-and-white television. Color television was available, but few could afford it back then. And you can forget cable, which had never even been heard of.

More changes were on the horizon, and we were due to leave for Utah in order for Lester to pursue his master's degree. A professor from Utah State University with whom Lester worked during a brief stint at the Brookings Institute had taken a great interest in Lester's career. After arranging admission and accommodation, we were to be on our way at the end of summer with my husband starting his graduate studies in the fall.

As I said, his behavior was changing and mood swings were not unusual, most of which I chalked up to work pressure and tiredness. Prior to leaving, he and some guys from the office decided to go out one night. It was in the middle of the workweek and I was a little worried; however, he promised to return home early. Unable to sleep, I feared drinking and driving, traffic accidents, all manner of things, until I dozed off around 1:30 A.M., exhausted. Not long after this, I heard the chain door fastener moving back and forth. It was 2:00 A.M. Frightened, I thought someone might be trying to break in. Usually Lester rang the doorbell or knocked on the door. None of this was happening.

Picking up enough courage to investigate the source of the problem, I discovered it was indeed Lester. Without thinking, I yelled at him, all the pent-up worry hurling toward him all at once. I felt entitled to it. I watched him for several minutes before finally letting him into the apartment.

Without saying anything, he picked up Casey's playpen that I kept in the middle of the living room and hurled it at me. Fortunately, I turned around very quickly, so the playpen only hit the left side of my back.

The excruciating pain knocked me to the floor, made from steel with mesh sides, the frame struck from my left shoulder down to my waist. Without saying a word, Lester rushed past me with no consideration as to how badly he had hurt me. Unable to sleep well because of the pain, I cried quietly and lay on the couch, bewildered.

The next day, while I was showering, I felt a huge lump on the left side of my back, which was painful to the touch. I checked it in the bathroom mirror, and my whole left back was not only swollen but also black and blue. I don't bruise easily, so I knew I was injured pretty badly. Lester, in the meantime, went about his business as if nothing happened. He never asked if I was hurt and never apologized for hitting me with the playpen. This was the beginning of the physical and emotional abuse that I would experience for the ten years I was married to him.

Years after, I happened to sit down one afternoon, taking a break from household duties, when I came across *The Oprah Winfrey Show*. Highlighting domestic violence, she repeated, "If he hits you once, he will hit you again." It was as though a light bulb flashed on inside my head. This was for real. I had not made any of it up. My bruises were real. The thing that happened to me had a name. For the first time, I felt validated. Love would not solve the problem, like many women believe. I could not love the anger out of him. Like thousands of women, I thought it would never happen again. And here I was, being told that chances are it would.

In August, we headed to Utah as planned. I was to find a job, as Lester's fellowship did not cover living expenses. I was never given a choice regarding work; he simply requested the personnel office to find something for me.

Eventually, a position was found in Brigham City, Utah, a full thirty-minute drive from Logan, where Utah State University was located. Angry, I asked him to consult me first prior to making plans for me. Enraged, he accused me of not wanting him to succeed. Blood draining from my face, I watched his anger in terror and wondered when all this aggression would hurl toward me. He was a controlling man, something I had no idea at that time how to handle. But I loved him, in spite of everything. I wanted him to succeed. Enough to keep moving around with this guy! Anyway, I had Casey to think about and knew she needed her father.

I took the job in Brigham City, despite my initial reservations. Elevated to a secretarial position, I now made more money. This hopefully would make my husband happy by showing him how much I wanted him to succeed. After he finished his studies, I also thought he would help me with going back to school. So with Casey in daycare a few blocks from my office, I began my new career.

## Chapter 4

Always thinking about the welfare and safety of Lester, I decided it would be best to move closer to the university so he would not have to travel late at night when he had classes in the evenings. I also was very concerned about the treacherous and dangerous roads during the winter months. So I discussed my concerns with him, and he was very much in favor of moving to Logan.

We moved two months later from Brigham City to Logan, where we found an apartment that was located five blocks from the university. We also found a highly rated daycare center for Casey, which was located three blocks from our apartment. Before our move to Logan, I found an advertisement about a man with a van that transported people from Logan to Brigham City and back every day. I was ever so lucky to find that he had room for me and that the cost was minimal.

Since I left for work before Casey woke up, we arranged to have Lester feed Casey breakfast and get her ready for the daycare center during the week. Once I got home from work, I took over caring for the family, which included making dinner, washing clothes, cleaning the house, and bathing and putting Casey to bed. Being the breadwinner, I was burdened with so many tasks that I always felt tired. Weekends were especially tiresome, since I did all the household chores because Lester never offered to help. In fact, when we first got married, he said he could not help with the household chores because his friends, relatives, and family would make fun of him. He also said the women in his own family did the housework. My own father never lifted a hand to help with the household chores or cook, so I did not bother to debate the issue with him.

In looking back to those days, I get sad and angry at the same time. How can anyone not be willing to help a spouse, especially when that spouse is working to support the family? I should have never accepted such nonsense. I encourage every young workingwoman today to request and, if necessary, demand they get help with the household chores from her husband.

After settling in Logan, I encouraged Lester to study at the university library so he could study in a quiet place. He would leave immediately after dinner either to study at the library or attend an evening class. He usually came home around 11:00 P.M. and sometimes around midnight. It was not until years later I found out that he was not studying at the library and did not have evening classes. He spent his time visiting other students or playing pool at the University Student Center. He had a lot of free time on his hands but never bothered to get a part-time job. His fellowship did not cover much beyond his tuition and books, so it was my job to support the family.

One evening, I came home to find him very unhappy. I asked what was wrong, but he did not answer me. Instead he let Casey out to play on the lawn in front of our apartment. He grabbed me by the arm and dragged me into the bedroom, where he raped me. I fought as hard as I could but was not able to free myself. I remember screaming as loudly as I could, and I am very sure the neighbors heard me. The apartments were all slab level, and the architectural acoustics were not very good. There were four apartments on one side and four on the other side with a narrow strip of lawn between them. After raping me, he left without saying a word.

I curled up into a ball and cried my heart out. Once I finished crying, I went to get Casey while praying that she had not wandered off into the street. I was always afraid of someone stealing her or that she would walk into the street going after one of the cats in our neighborhood. She loved cats and dogs and still does to this day.

Worried sick, I found Casey chatting with a young couple on their porch at the end apartment. I brought her home and fed her dinner, but I did not eat since I was no longer hungry.

As always, life went on as usual the next day. There were no explanations or apologies from Lester for what he did to me. I did not ask any questions because I did not want to start an argument. That would have given him an excuse to take off in the car and disappear for days.

Despite the abuses, I wanted us to have a good Christmas. Since we did not have much money, I withdrew the retirement funds I had earned while working for the federal government in Washington. With the money, I was able to purchase Christmas gifts for all of us. At my request, my sister from Salt Lake City spent the Christmas holiday with us. We had a good time, and I did not do too badly in fixing Christmas dinner.

In March of the New Year, I became pregnant again. I was happy about having a brother or sister for Casey. She was also excited and often listened to my stomach to see if she could hear anything.

Lester completed his first year of the two-year master's program in early spring and got a job as a consultant that summer. Since most of the work was for a company located in Denver, Colorado, he was gone for most of that summer.

## The Forgotten American

In the fall of our second year in Logan, Lester and I had a big argument on a Saturday morning. The argument was over something that he considered minute: helping with the household chores. After the argument he took off in the car to parts unknown, which was his usual routine. Lester did not return home that Saturday night or the entire week. Casey and I were left with no car and very little food. Fortunately, this was the week that I planned to keep Casey home with me, so being without a car was not such a big deal, but that was hardly the point.

I had just resigned from my secretarial position in Brigham City and had accepted a job in Logan the previous week. The position I accepted was to work as a counselor/tutor for the Indian College Program at Utah State University, which had just been implemented. I had arranged my resignation so that I could care for my daughter for one full week before reporting to my new job at the university. I was getting ready to go to the grocery store to replenish our food supplies when Lester and I got into the argument.

Casey was now three and half years old, so she was able to walk with me several times to the mini-grocery store. The store was about four city blocks from home. She did request for us to sit down on the sidewalk curb to rest on one trip. On the other two trips, she seemed to be so happy to be outside that she chatted and skipped alongside me to and from the store. For his anger and inconsideration, ultimately, it was absent husband who was losing out. I had Casey and all her joy.

After several days, I became very worried about Lester and also about my unborn baby. I did not know whether Lester was dead or alive. I was now six months pregnant and was beginning to have unusual pain in my left side and needed to see my doctor. I finally swallowed my pride and called the wife of the professor who had gotten Lester into the master's program. I wanted to find out if her husband knew his whereabouts. She did not want to talk on the phone and offered to come to my home the following day.

As promised, the professor's wife came to my home on a Friday as she promised. She said she spoke with her husband, and he did not know anything about Lester's disappearance. She kept quizzing me on our life and wanted to know if we were having marital problems. I did not discuss any of our problems with her, but I did tell her about the big argument. I also said we had minor problems that many young couples face in their first few years of marriage. I asked that our discussions on my home life be held in confidence, and she assured me they would be. After she left, I started searching for Lester by telephone.

During the week, we were alone without a car and could not go anywhere. My sister from Salt Lake City called on Thursday and told me about a children's play being held at the big indoor stadium in Salt Lake City. The play was *Snow White and the Seven Dwarfs*. I told her that Casey and I were alone. Before I could tell her that I had no way of getting to the play, she offered to pick us up on Saturday morning.

It was nice to get out of the house at last, to be in a different environment and to simply have a good time. The only sad part was the strap on Casey's only dress shoe broke. It was so sad to have to carry her while all the other children ran about with their parents. However, it seemed not to bother her too much. During the play, she clapped her hands constantly.

At one point during the performance, the witch turned to the audience and asked, "Who wants the apple?" Casey did not hesitate to yell out at the top of her voice, "I want the apple, Witch!" Everyone turned to look at her and smiled.

After the play, my sister took us home to Logan and spent the night with us. She wanted to know if Lester was away on a consulting trip. I lied and told her that he had to make a quick trip to Boulder, Colorado, and that the car was parked at the airport. I did not tell my sister about the argument or that Lester rushed off with the car and had not yet returned home. That evening I wanted to tell her about the emotional and physical abuse I endured while living in Logan, but I did not. It was too embarrassing for me to talk about it, and I was afraid I would break down and cry. Also, I was now six months pregnant, and I wanted to keep our family together for the sake of Casey and our unborn child. At the time, I thought by being a helpful and good wife, our family would stay together for life.

The next day, my sister went back to Salt Lake City. Her departure left me feeling incredibly lonely. The fun had with my sister only served to highlight the loneliness I felt within my marriage. I was also concerned about Lester since I still had no idea to his whereabouts.

The following day, Monday, I went to my new job at Utah State University. Before the day was over, my new supervisor informed me that there were rumors on campus that a young married couple was having problems with their marriage. He said he heard at the faculty meeting that morning that the husband was a graduate student and asked me if I knew them. I said I did not know them, but obviously the rumor was about my life. This professor's wife, who assured me our discussion was confidential, had gone back to campus and informed not only her husband but also other faculty members. I never trusted the professor or his wife again, and I never communicated with them again.

A couple days after the visit from the professor's wife, I managed to locate Lester at his mother's home in South Dakota. When asked why he had left both his pregnant wife and young daughter with neither food nor transportation, he was unable to answer the question.

The following Saturday, he came home and, head buried in his hands, listened to me as I discussed the future of our family and unborn child. As he pretended to cry, I wished there were tears, but there were none I could see. Everything was an act. At the end of the day, he still had one year of graduate work left and needed my assistance as his financial provider.

Today, I would not hesitate to leave and start concentrating on my own education and career. I would turn to organizations that help women in difficult situations. Being young with a young child kept me in bondage back in those days. I look back today and see that I could have accomplished so much more for my daughter and me if I had left him. I wasted so many years on my marriage—caring for him, encouraging him every step of the way, recommending ways to accomplish his future goals, and even helping him with his educational studies.

That year was full of emotional, more than physical, abuse. I rarely saw Lester except on weekends. He was always gone in the evenings and disappeared from time to time but always had an excuse that was connected with his studies. What is so sad is that he never apologized for any wrong actions he took. He would at times tell me that things would be better tomorrow, and I believed him.

In November of that year, our last one in Logan, I suffered a miscarriage. But to look at my husband, you would never have known it. Hardly ever at home, he provided little to no support. Casey did not want to believe our baby was gone and often asked to listen to my stomach. Finally, though, she accepted the baby was gone and was now an angel in heaven. I believe the stress of my marriage caused the miscarriage. It was such a sad time.

## Chapter 5

Upon completion of all of his academic courses in the spring of the second year, Lester was offered a summer job in Pine Ridge, South Dakota. He had not yet completed his master's thesis for the program but was given approval by the university to submit it anytime within the following year. Once again I had to quit another job and uproot my daughter from the friends she had made. I did not want to move to a desolate area where racism was rampant. I knew in my heart that I would not be able to make friends in such a place. I also felt some resentment toward my husband but again told myself that his success and happiness would make us happy. So I resigned from my job, and we headed to Pine Ridge a week after school ended. We searched for housing for one solid week in Pine Ridge, but nothing was available. There were no apartments or houses for rent in this tiny town. The organization that hired my husband for the summer did not lift a hand to help us find a home for the summer, either.

After exhausting all avenues in our search for a home in Pine Ridge, we started searching in Nebraska. We searched in a nearby town called Chadron, Nebraska, about fifty miles away from Pine Ridge. All we could find in this small farm town was a small-furnished trailer on the outskirts of the city limits. The trailer had one air conditioner in the bedroom window, but it did not provide much cool air in the bedroom or anywhere else in the trailer. We had planned to rent a furnished apartment or house for the summer.

Once the summer job was fulfilled, we planned to move to Los Angeles the last week of August. At least it was only for a short time. In the fall, Lester was due to start his Ph.D. program at the University of California in the School of Management. Another move, but I looked forward to it.

I was pregnant again. This time hoping for a better outcome, being cooped up in a stuffy old trailer fell far short of comfortable. As miserable as I was during this summer, I was determined to go full term and have this baby.

## Paula B. Compton

There were no children Casey's age in this tiny neighborhood, so she had no playmates. There were only two trailers in the neighborhood, and the other trailer near us had older children who sometimes asked her to play. Being much younger, some of them were not very kind to her at times, so she would just come home. I really did not want her playing with the older children, so I spent much of the time playing with here in the trailer or outside when it was not so hot. Since Lester had to drive to his job in Pine Ridge every day, we were left without transportation. In fact, we were cut off to the outside world five days a week and sometimes six days a week. To make matters worse, there was no telephone in the trailer. We purchased a small black-and-white television from the local furniture store, thinking we could at least watch television. Unfortunately, the television reception was bad most of the time.

Chadron was not a place I wanted to live, but I had no choice due to lack of housing in Pine Ridge. I am sure race relations are much better today, but back in the early 1970s, the town of Chadron was about ninety-eight percent white, and race relations were bad. Many people were not accepting of anyone who was not Caucasian. They looked down on all minorities but especially on Native Americans since they represented a large portion of the population in South Dakota. Back in the 1970s, racism was still very rampant in the western states, where there were large populations of Native Americans. For Native Americans, it was like being African American and living in the South.

I still remember a lady in the grocery store who looked at me and commented really loudly that she would rather have a "black" living next door to her than a "Native American." This lady neither lived near me nor did she know me, but I guess stating such a hateful statement made her feel superior. I seriously doubt she would be accepting of an African American or any other person of color living next door to her. She appeared to be an uneducated redneck.

Life at home was not much better. Lester would often stay in Pine Ridge on Friday evening and at various times during the week. His famous and only story was that the "boys and him" went to a bar to drink and play pool, and it was too late to drive home. Without a telephone, it was not possible for him to call us to let us know that he would be spending the night in Pine Ridge. We also could not call anyone in Pine Ridge to find out where he was staying or to find out if he was okay.

One morning in the last week of July, I decided to leave Lester without a car in Chadron so he would find out what it was like to be stranded in a desolate place. I decided to go visit my sister in Salt Lake City. He had come home around five that morning and was scheduled to fly to Colorado with his boss that morning, which I did not know. While he was sleeping, I quickly dressed Casey, packed a few things, and drove away to Utah. I felt light and greatly relieved while I was driving away from Chadron.

We arrived in Salt Lake early in the evening, and my sister was so surprised and happy to see us. As usual, she did not ask if anything was wrong, and I did not tell her the problems and hardships I was dealing with while living in Chadron. We stayed for several days in Utah before I called Lester at his office. The office secretary said he was on a business trip to Fort Duchesne, Utah, and that she would let him know I called when he called the office around 4:00 P.M. I said to let him know that Casey and I were fine and left my sister's number with her.

That evening I received a call from him, and he wanted us to return home. He wanted us to meet him at the motel where he was staying on Friday evening. He said that he would be completing his business that day and wanted all of us to drive home together. He made all kinds of promises and made a pledge to come home every evening during the remaining three weeks on the job. I agreed to the plan since Casey missed her dad, and we really had no place to go. We met him at his hotel on Friday evening, and we all drove back to Chadron the next day. Looking back now, it would have been much better for Casey and me to remain in our apartment in Logan, where she at least had friends and we knew the neighbors. I could have at least kept my job for a while longer before moving to Los Angeles.

The last week in August, Lester came home early on Wednesday and wanted us to spend a couple of days in Pine Ridge with some friends. On the second day in Pine Ridge, I became ill and had to be taken to the local hospital there in Pine Ridge. The doctors examined me and said my unborn baby was fine but wanted to keep me overnight for further observation. I stayed that night and went to the home of the people we were staying with the next morning. Lester made his round of goodbyes in the neighborhood that day.

We left for home in Chadron on a Monday morning to pack up and leave for Los Angeles. On the way home, I said I was very much looking forward to living in Los Angeles. We were somewhere near a ranch and several farms when I spoke about my excitement. Without a word, Lester opened the car door on my side and started pushing me out the door. I hung on for dear life since the car was going at least seventy miles an hour. He kept pushing me, and Casey was crying and screaming at the top of her lungs in the back seat. I was clutching the seat cushion underneath me while crying and yelling, "Stop!" I gave up my fight to hang on when the car slowed down, and I just tumbled out of the car.

Fortunately, I landed safely on some tall but soft prairie grass. I picked myself up and ran as fast as I could toward a barn nearby. I thought he was going to kill me, so I hid in the barn. I saw him running toward the barn, and Casey was in the car, still crying and screaming her lungs out. He found me crouching near a bale of hay, and I thought that was the end of my life, but he softly said, "Don't be scared. I won't hurt you. Your daughter is crying and needs you." He did not say, "I am sorry," and he did not say, "our daughter." Instead he said, "your daughter." He did wipe my tears and led me back to the car.

Trapped, I might well have been a caged animal fighting for freedom. With no money, no job, and no friends, there was no one to turn to for advice and comfort. I remember crying softly on the way home. Sad for me and sad that Casey had been forced to witness her mother's terror at the hands of her father.

Once home, he attempted to explain his behavior by telling me that he lost his mind for a moment because he really did not want to leave the area just yet. He also said he did not want to enter the Ph.D. program. I said that was fine with me but that I could and would not stay in this part of the country anymore. Before I completed my sentence, he said he did want to get his Ph.D. and that he was just upset about leaving the job and people he was helping. Within the next five minutes, he made a decision to go to Los Angeles, and we packed and left Chadron for good. I often wonder today why I stayed with Lester knowing that I could have died on the highway. The only answer that I can come up with is that it was for the sake of our unborn child and Casey.

## Chapter 6

Since we had left our primary belongings in Logan during Lester's short summer employment, we arrived back in Logan ready for the moving company. After they were done packing our furniture and household items, we then got back on the road once more, this time headed for Los Angeles. It was a Saturday afternoon, and since the trip promised to be a long one, we decided to spend the night in Vegas. At around 7:00 P.M., Lester left Casey and me in order to hit the tables.

I awoke in the morning only to realize he had not returned to the hotel room, so at around 9:00 A.M. on Saturday, after him being missing the entire night, I finally started calling around. Shortly afterward, he returned to the hotel, claiming getting caught up in the gambling games. He had gambled all night. I never thought to ask where he had been all night. He claimed to have lost some money but made it back, plus an additional two hundred dollars. A lot of money back then.

Looking back, I think he might have arranged to meet someone at the casino, most likely a woman. But I was so naïve back then that something like that never crossed my mind, as unbelievable as that sounds.

I was happy to leave the hotel. I didn't gamble, so I had no further use for the heat of Vegas other than a place for Casey and me to eat and sleep before heading on to Los Angeles, where I looked forward to the opportunities such a cosmopolitan city could bring myself and our children. It was early evening on a beautiful Sunday by the time we reached Los Angeles and the motel we were to spend the night in. Close to the university, it made it easy for Lester to pop over to the campus the following morning and register for his classes, in addition to obtaining his doctoral fellowship funds for tuition and living expenses.

Happy to be in a new location, the change of scene suggested a chance to start over. No matter what road I took, Casey, the unborn baby, and I would be fine. They were the highest priority in my life.

Living in Los Angeles can be expensive, so we expanded our search for an apartment toward the San Fernando Valley area. Over the hill from Los Angeles, it was about twenty minutes from the university, in light traffic. However, anyone who has ever spent any time in L.A. knows the chance of driving in light traffic is about as likely as an L.A. snowstorm.

We found a very nice apartment in a small complex managed by an elderly lady and her daughter. They were very friendly and kind and made me feel at home. The climate was warm mixed with a cool breeze from the Pacific Ocean. The people were very pleasant. Everything seemed to be different from our previous location. I was so happy to be living in Los Angeles with all the wonderful amenities that were not available to us in Nebraska.

As scheduled, the moving van arrived, enabling us to move into our new apartment just three days after our arrival in town. Eager to feel fit and healthy for my new baby, I made sure I walked for thirty minutes a day, taking advantage of Casey's outdoor time on her tricycle.

About three weeks after we arrived in Los Angeles, I got very sick and knew something was terribly wrong with my pregnancy. It was around 3:00 P.M. when the pain in my stomach got really bad, so I called the university to have them contact Lester in one of his afternoon classes. In the meantime, I called the nearest hospital and got advice on various actions I should take until I could get to the hospital. I was very scared and even thought I might bleed to death before Lester arrived home. Fortunately, the university's Security and Emergency Office personnel were able to find Lester within half an hour. He called me as soon as he received the emergency message and said he was on his way home. As soon as he got home, he rushed me to the emergency room at the hospital.

After examining me, the doctors informed Lester and me they believed the fetus was dead and needed to perform emergency surgery right away. Apparently, the fetus had been dead for some time, and I thought back to the doctors at the hospital in South Dakota, where I had been just weeks earlier with similar symptoms only to send me packing with the "the baby is developing normally" tagline.

I was angry and upset. I had tried to take care of myself and felt as though my body had somehow betrayed me. Then I thought of Lester, the stress of his continue absences, the constant moving around, the constant fear his temper might ignite at any moment. And the time he pushed me out of the car. All these things surely had conspired to where I lay now, in the hospital; in pain and being told I should be thankful I had not died also, from poisoning. But there was little time to reflect. Before I could give everything another thought, I was being whisked to the pre-op room and prepped for surgery. Following the surgery, the doctor who performed the surgery came to examine me once again. During the conversation afterward, he confirmed my fears. That stress and lifestyle can affect the outcome of a pregnancy and miscarriages were particularly hard on the body. He finished by advising Lester and I think very seriously before committing to having another child and the outcome for my health, should this happen again, may not be so positive. I wanted to cry but had to be strong for Casey. This was a second time she had lost a baby brother or sister.

I shared the doctor's advice with Lester, who for once appeared to be concerned and said I should make the decision since I was the one who had to carry the baby for nine months. Based on what had taken place in my personal life since I got married and what the doctor had said, I decided it was not wise to have another child. I informed Lester that I decided not to have any more children, and he accepted my decision.

The following week, I decided it was time to make some changes to my plans for the future. I started searching for local universities and colleges located close to home with the intention of attending. I wanted one that was very close to home so I could continue to care for Casey and still be able to attend school. I also started searching for scholarships that could provide funding both for tuition and living expenses.

After establishing a plan, I informed Lester of my decision to go back to school and what I had to do before I could enroll. He did not say much but appeared to be happy with my decision. I am assuming it was because I was planning on obtaining funds not only for tuition but also for living expenses.

I was accepted by California State University in Northridge (Cal State University) for the spring semester. I selected Cal State Northridge because it was only fifteen minutes from home and also because it accepted most of my college credits from the University of Oklahoma and University of New Mexico. Since I was able to transfer all of my previous college credits, I was left with only two years of college work. As an enrolled member of the Navajo Tribe, I had applied for a scholarship to its scholarship office and was awarded one for tuition and living expenses. Members of the Navajo Tribe who still reside on the reservation are located in the four corners of Colorado, Utah, New Mexico, and Arizona. The Navajo Tribe is one of the 562 federally recognized tribes in the United States.

I enrolled for the second semester in January 1972 to complete my undergraduate program. My courses were arranged to enable me to take care of Casey, who was now four years old and in pre-kindergarten. School for her normally ended at 4:00 P.M. Casey had constantly begged us to attend school, so shortly after my miscarriage we enrolled her in a pre-kindergarten school, which was located two blocks from home.

I have never seen a child who was so eager to go to school as Casey. She now has several college degrees but still enjoys taking courses at various universities in the evenings when she is not traveling abroad on business.

That semester, Casey and I spent many days and weekends alone. Lester would pick a fight and then disappear for days. Sometimes he took the car and left Casey and me stranded for days. During these times, I walked Casey to school, and then I caught the city bus to school, which stopped very near the university campus. Fortunately, the pre-kindergarten school was within walking distance from home. In the afternoon, I also took the bus home and walked down to Casey's school to pick her up. And we slowly walked home together.

When Lester did return home, he never said where he had been and never apologized for leaving us stranded. In fact, he never even asked how we got to school or the grocery store. I did not bother to question him either since Casey was always so happy to see her dad. He was also very happy to see her and would tell her that he loved her very much and to never forget it. During those rough times, I promised myself that no matter how bad things got, I would finish my undergraduate degree and go on to graduate school.

For some unknown reason, I knew that one of the California universities would select me for admission to its master's program. However, I was not so sure about finding funding for the master's program, but I was more determined than ever to continue my education beyond a bachelor's degree. I studied hard for all my classes at Cal State that spring semester. At the end of the semester, I was very pleased to learn that I had made the dean's honor list.

## Chapter 7

That summer Lester and I both got a job in Sacramento. Once again we paid our rent for the summer and left everything in the apartment. We enrolled Casey at a children's all-day camp near the place where we were employed. Casey always enjoyed being with other children since she did not have any siblings. The summer for her started out with lots of fun and laughter.

Everything was going pretty well for all of us until one evening, when Lester said he had to go to the office to work and would be home by 9:00 P.M. He did not come home that Friday evening. When he did finally return on Saturday morning, we had a big argument, blaming one another for various things that happened in our marriage. He started to jerk me around and was ready to hit me when I said, "Do you want Casey and me to leave?" and he said, "Do whatever you want, and maybe you should leave."

After Lester told me to do what I wanted, I decided to fly to Salt Lake City to visit my sister. I packed a few things for Casey and myself and called a taxicab to go to the airport. I knew I did not have much money, but I thought I could depend on my own savings account that I set up for emergencies. Well, it turned out that the cost of the flight for the two of us was way more than what I had in my special account. I was so sad that we could not leave the unhappy situation. We stayed at the airport until noon to make sure Lester was gone and then took a taxicab back to the apartment. I knew he would not come home that Saturday evening, and he did not. He probably thought we were long gone and likely did not care.

Sunday evening, he arrived home with a man who was in town doing business with the company we were working for that summer. Lester did not say one word as he entered the apartment and did not bother to introduce the man. After changing his clothes, he left with the stranger and didn't return again until Monday morning. And as usual, he refused to talk about his activities during the time he was gone from home. He didn't even want to discuss our marriage.

In spite of Lester, my own outlook was expanded, and instead of being constantly stuck in the apartment, there were some good times in the form of new friendships at the office. Often we would go whitewater rafting, hiking, and other outdoor activities.

## Chapter 8

One month before we were to go back for school in Los Angeles, Lester said he was offered a job as president of a newly established college for Native Americans and Hispanics. The college, called D-Q University, was founded in September 1971 and is located seven miles west of the University of California in Davis. The full name of the college is Deganawidah-Quetzalcoatl. Deganawidah is the name of a Native American man who founded the Iroquois Confederacy, and Quetzalcoatl is the name of a major Aztec god.

Lester informed me one afternoon at lunch that he was going to accept the position and that I could enroll at the University of California (UC) in Davis for the fall semester. It looked like I did not have a choice in the matter, so like a good wife, I agreed to do so. I was able to enroll at UC Davis without any trouble, since the university recognized Cal State as a sister school. However, UC Davis was based on a quarter, and not semester, system like Cal State, so I knew I would lose some credits once I transferred back to Cal State.

By now my daily life, jobs, and school had been interrupted so many times to accommodate Lester's career and academic education. Being young, ambitious, and having a great desire to finish my academic training, I did not feel cheated of anything in life at the time. Looking back, I see that I had given up so much for my husband. Despite my sacrifices, he was never thankful for them and, quite often, put the blame on me for some things that went wrong in his life. He blamed me for not seeing his mother as much as he wanted. The truth was we visited his mother way more than my parents. In fact, during our years together, we visited my parents only eight times, and way more than eight did we visit his mother.

That fall of 1972, I entered UC Davis to continue my undergraduate studies. Lester also started his work as president of D-Q University that fall. I enrolled Casey in the first grade in a school close to our home. The school was so close that she could walk to and from school. She begged to walk to and from school by herself, so I would stand on the front lawn until she went into the school building. I set up my course schedule so that I could leave for school after she entered the school building and arrive home in time to watch her walk home from school.

Lester was hard at work preparing D-Q University to become an accredited school, so we hardly saw him that year. Rarely did he make it home for dinner. After one month of not seeing him at the dinner table, we both agreed I should not save dinner for him anymore. I was also busy that year taking care of Casey and studying late into the night during the school week. Casey would take time to clean up for her dad in the evenings, believing he would make it home for dinner. She would wet the front of her long hair and comb it so she would look pretty for her him. He normally came home long after she had gone to bed.

I still get very sad today when I think of her getting ready for her dad or at times asking me to drive her to the university to see him before she went to bed. I would tell her that he always checked on her when he got home and gave her many kisses while she slept. She loved hearing that and would smile really big.

During the one year at Davis, there was not only physical, but also emotional, abuse from Lester. The physical abuse occurred once in a while, but the emotional abuse seemed to be a constant. By emotional, I mean Lester was rarely home, and when he was home, we did not do much as a family. He would usually get home from work after 9:00 P.M. and sometimes after midnight. In addition, he would quite often have to go to the office on Saturdays. When he was home on weekends, we usually got into arguments, and his solution was always so shove me around or even hit me with his fist. I always covered my face when he started shoving me around, so when he hit me it would land on my back. I made sure I got away from him as quickly as possible so that the pounding of my body did not continue.

As soon as I ran away from him, he would make a mad dash for the door, slam it shut, and speed away in the car. Once he was gone, Casey and I would go to her room and lie down together. After resting for a while, she would get her toys and start playing near me, and I would either watch or play with her. If I fell asleep, I would wake up to her tiny hand touching me below my nose. I asked her one-day why she did that, and she said to make sure I was still breathing. I assured her that I would always be well and fine to take care of her, and I kept that promise.

One Sunday morning when Lester was home, he wanted to go to church. While getting ready for church, we got into an argument over something minor. I do not remember to this day what the argument was about. I stopped arguing and turned around to finish getting ready when I felt a very sharp pain at the top of my head. I turned around and saw him holding one boot. He had hit me. The tip of the boot sunk into the skin of my head. The pain was so bad that I started to cry. Blood dripped down my face. He turned away and started walking down the hallway, and I knew he was going to speed away in the car. I screamed at him to take me to the hospital emergency room before he ran off. Casey started screaming and

## The Forgotten American

crying so hard that he stopped and said, "Get in the car."

He took me to the emergency room as I requested. He never said a word to Casey or me on the way to the hospital or on the way home. Today, I wonder why he wanted to go to church when he was so full of anger and maybe even hate. When we got to the emergency room, he immediately left the area and did not bother to get me registered at the desk. The washcloth I was holding to my head was completely soaked with blood when we arrived at the hospital. The receptionist said, "Oh, you poor thing, what happened?" I said the garage door hit me, and the receptionist quickly gave me a form to complete.

Within minutes, a kind-looking doctor came out and took me to his examining room. The doctor said the gash in my head was pretty deep and wanted to know what happened. I was too embarrassed to tell him the truth, so I said the garage door malfunctioned and hit me. I also was afraid they would report the incident to the police. I had a six-inch gap at the top of my head, which was extremely painful. The doctor did an excellent job in sewing up the cut. Today, you cannot see the scar unless you use a microscope to find it. He gave me some medication for the pain and some antibiotics to take for the next ten days. The doctor also wanted to see me for a follow-up exam in a few days. Casey was very happy to receive a red sucker from the doctor.

Casey and I found Lester walking around in the hallway. He never showed any remorse for what he did. I don't believe to this day that he knows the definition of the word "apology." As soon as we drove into the driveway of our home, Casey and I quickly got out of the car. Instead of following us into the house, Lester remained in the car and drove away at full speed. Not once did he look back to make sure we even had the key to get into the house.

Casey and I ate a small lunch, and I told her that I had to rest for the afternoon. I was getting very sleepy from the pain pills, so we went in to her bedroom to rest. She was not allowed to have a television in her room, so she decided to play with her toys on the bed while I rested. I fell asleep within a few minutes and woke up as Casey was holding her tiny right hand under my nose to feel my breath. I told her I was fine and that by looking at my chest she could also see that I was breathing. But I guess she preferred to feel my breath, which she did for the next few years.

Later that afternoon, we watched a children's show on television in the living room. That evening for dinner, Casey helped me prepare hamburgers—one of Casey's favorite foods through her young adult years. She wanted to have a picnic in the backyard, so we took our burgers and corn chips out to the patio and ate under the peach tree. She was happy and skipping as we took our food out to the patio. I was so happy to see her skipping and laughing that evening.

The following week, I threw myself deeper into my studies and swore that I would get into graduate school to study for my master's degree. Lester never returned home that week, so we had no car to get around. I watched Casey walk to school, as she and I had agreed when school started. I took either the campus bus to school, which stopped down the street from our house, or walked if I had enough time. If we needed small grocery items, Casey and I would walk to the grocery store located about three blocks from our house.

On Friday evening, I had put Casey to bed and was studying at the kitchen table when, lo and behold, Lester walked into the house. As he usually did after his absences, he went straight to the bedroom without saying anything to me. I could hear him putting his clothes in the dirty clothes hamper and hanging up his jacket. After taking a shower, he went straight to bed. I continued studying until midnight, reminding myself that no matter what happened I would stay in school and graduate with honors. I also said very softly, "Graduate school is possible, so start planning for it."

The next day, life at home went on as if nothing terrible had happened. Casey, of course, was so happy to see her dad that she followed him around everywhere. He played with her all Saturday morning and then took her with him to run his errands. And like a good wife, I spent the day cleaning the house, grocery shopping, and cooking for the family. While doing my chores, I prayed for strength and guidance.

The latter part of March of that year, Lester resigned from D-Q University due to the bickering of not only the board of directors but also some Hispanic and Native-American organizations. I sensed long ago that there was too much bad politics among the people who were responsible for managing the university. The Hispanics and Native Americans who made up the board of directors were at war with one another. The bickering was over the accreditation and long-term management of the newly established university. In addition, they were trying to micromanage Lester's daily planning and management of the university.

I was not aware that he resigned until news reporters started calling my home and knocking on my door one afternoon. Although I knew he was facing all kinds of political hassles by the board of directors, I was not aware that he was planning to resign. It was that week when I found out that some journalists do not always report information accurately. I realized very quickly that statements made by people are distorted and taken out of context by some of them.

I had no desire to talk with the journalists who were calling or knocking on my door that week. It became necessary for me to close the drapes, close all outside doors, and take the telephone off the hook for a couple of days. The first day I did respond to a couple of journalists, who not only misquoted me but also took most of my comments out of context. My name and comments were televised that evening and splashed across the local newspapers the next day. I was too embarrassed to go to my classes, so I stayed away from the university campus for one full day.

That week was a very devastating week for me. I received threatening calls and written notes that were filled with hate. No one who called by telephone

## The Forgotten American

identified himself or herself, but I could tell some were from the Native-American and Hispanic communities. Although these people never identified themselves, their accents always gave them away. One message left at my door said my family should have fear since life can easily be taken away. Another said, "Your family will be destroyed unless you quit making statements to the reporters." Another message said my family must leave the area if we wanted to live. I never went through so much agony that week, and I swore that I would never take a job that involved politics.

The sad and frightening thing about this whole affair was that Casey and I were left alone to fend for ourselves. Lester did not even bother to call me and let me know that he resigned and to see if we were safe. I found out through the news on TV and newspaper that he left the area after he resigned and could not be reached. I wanted to quit school and leave the area as well, but I did not. I had made a commitment several years back that no matter how bad things got; I was going to finish my college education. So I stayed and continued to go to my classes. Things did die down after two weeks, and my daily activities were almost back to normal.

Lester did finally return home the weekend after he resigned. Prior to resigning, he evidently had arranged to perform consulting work for a company in Denver. This company was owned by one of his relatives. And of course he did not consult me about the job in Denver until after he resigned. Two weeks later, he left for Denver, promising to call every week and check on us.

I felt so bad for what he had gone through at D-Q University, but I did warn him about what could happen when he told me he was going to accept the job. At the same time, I also began to resent him for taking advantage of me. My education and career were never considered as important as his. He just took for granted that I would agree to his every desire and that I would be there to take care of Casey and him. As her father, he not only had the financial responsibility to care for her but also the daily responsibilities that go into raising a child, and at those things, he failed miserably.

Both Casey and I had been left alone so much that we did not miss him a whole lot when he left for Denver. He did call every week to check on us. I had started spring quarter when my husband resigned from D-Q University. That quarter, I had a very candid professor of sociology. Everyone, especially the girls, said he was not only a very hard professor but also a racist. I grew up with racism, so I knew I probably would not get an A. Despite all the negative criticism, I decided I would make an attempt to get an A from this professor. The first day of class, he said everyone was expected to attend every session, and getting an A was not easy in his class.

I waited until Lester got settled in Denver to discuss my concerns on the topic of our family being uprooted continuously for his education and career. I informed him that if his education and career were the only important things in his life, I had no choice but to leave him. I also told him that I wanted to finish my education and wanted to start a real career. The distance between us helped me to discuss our problems and my desire to finish school as quickly as possible. I also told him that I wanted to give our daughter a stable environment that was more than a year here and there. Surprisingly, he listened, and he agreed with my plans and desires and agreed to stop uprooting us so often as in the past. I noticed immediately that he used the words "agree to stop uprooting us" and not "promise," which would have been more acceptable to me, but I let it pass.

The professor's racist thinking did not come out until the third week of school. He started in on Jewish people. I will always remember one very young, pretty Jewish girl who always contested his views on various races of people, especially Jewish people. I often felt it was a waste of precious class time since he would get all fired up and spend the next twenty minutes defending his views on the subject matter. The professor commented on the behavior and characteristic of every race in the United States, and of course, his comments were not complimentary.

On one memorable afternoon, the professor started making comments about Native Americans, and back in those days, we were called American Indians. He said he could not understand why most American Indians belonged to the Presbyterian Church when so many were very poor. He said that only the rich usually belonged to the Presbyterian Church. I could not dispute the information since he was correct on both points. The Presbyterian missionaries began working with Native tribes back in the early 1800s, and that is why many Native Americans are often identified as belonging to the Presbyterian Church. And, indeed, many are poor because of the reservation environment that white America created for them. Native Americans still living on Indian reservations have the highest unemployment rates in the United States.

I was rather disappointed that I received a B+ in the professor's class even though I made an A on the final exam. I assumed back then that the students were correct about the professor being a racist. My view of the professor changed once I entered the real working environment. I realized then that the professor was not only preparing us for the real world but was trying to give us the tools to survive in it. He was telling it like it is. That was the last quarter of school and my last year in Davis, California. I made the dean's honor list despite receiving the B+ in sociology from the professor.

## Chapter 9

Lester called a week before school ended at UC Davis and informed me that a newly established firm called "The American Indian Consortium" wanted to hire an administrative assistant for the summer. He said if I was interested, the director was ready to hire me. I did not hesitate for a moment to take the job.

The following week after school ended, I arranged with the owner of our leased home to sublease it for the summer. He was agreeable to the arrangement since the new tenants were parents of our next-door neighbors. Our neighbors had found out that we were leaving for the season, so they asked both the owner and me if the wife's parents could live there for the summer. She was expecting another child in mid-summer, and the grandparents were to help with the new baby and the other three children.

Lester flew home the week I finished school to drive us to Denver. We took only the clothes we would be wearing during the summer and left everything else in our leased home. The drive to Denver was long but a pleasant one. Driving through the mountains was so refreshing and exciting. The weather was much cooler than Davis. We went apartment hunting the next day, and we were very lucky to find a very new and clean one that met our budget. The apartment was located in a small apartment complex close to the Denver airport.

That same day we found a pre-kindergarten school for Casey that was located close to our apartment. People we knew in Denver rated this particular school as one of the best schools. She was very happy to go to the pre-kindergarten school because it was similar to the one she attended in Los Angeles.

I reported to work that week, and Lester went back to work with the company he joined back in March after resigning from D-Q University. Since the organization I joined was fairly new, it had only one director, one education specialist, and me, the administrative assistant. We all reported to the board of directors of the organization.

During my spare time in the office that summer, I drafted a personnel manual on the policies and procedures to be followed by "The American Indian Consortium." Since the organization was in its infancy stage, the work was light and easy for all of us. This allowed me to work on, and complete, the manual before returning to school at Cal State. I was happy to learn that it became the organization's official personnel manual. I was more than pleased and had a deep sense of accomplishment when my former boss of that organization called me in California to thank me for drafting the manual.

The summer months went by pretty fast. Lester stayed close to home except for one weekend when we argued over his foolish spending of our money. He disappeared for a couple of days but never revealed where he went. I also never asked where he went or what he did during his absence. By this time, I was just interested in completing my education and starting a career so I could leave if our married life did not improve. Despite the ups and downs of our marriage, I tried very hard to make it work the best I knew how. I knew in my heart that if I worked hard at making the marriage work and it did not work, I could walk away with a clear conscience. He might have sensed my plans because I don't remember any negative incidents that took place that summer except that one argument.

A funny thing did happen one evening that summer. Lester wanted Casey and me to go to the office with him since he had work to complete before the next day. On the elevator to his office, for some unknown reason, he said he was beginning to go bald and that I might leave him. I said in a joking manner that it would happen. He got very upset and said, "You want to leave me now that I am bald." I found that to be hilarious because he had lost only a few strands of hair but certainly was not bald. I stopped laughing and assured him that he was not yet bald and that I was not planning to leave him. All went well that evening and for the rest of the summer.

## Chapter 10

In mid-August of that year, we returned to Davis, packed our things, and then headed back to Los Angeles with the purpose of completing our education. Lester had one more year of course work in his doctoral program. I also had one more year to get my bachelor's degree. Since the courses I took were on a quarter basis at UC Davis, I lost some credits when they were transferred back to Cal State. Despite losing credits, I only had eighteen course units left to graduate.

My plan for the final spring semester was to do the following: spend more time with Casey, apply to several universities to work on my master's degree, and search for scholarships and fellowships for my master's program. Indeed I was able to spend more time with Casey, which I thoroughly enjoyed. I also applied to a couple of universities and several organizations for scholarships and fellowships for graduate school. And I received my bachelor's degree with honors from Cal State in June 1974.

I applied to only two schools for my master's program. The two schools I selected were the University of California at Los Angeles and Massachusetts Institute of Technology (MIT) in Cambridge, Massachusetts. The application for both schools had a section for identifying your race. This was on a volunteer basis, so an applicant did not have to identify his or her race if he or she did not want to do so. I chose not to identify my race because I did not want the selection committee to give me preferential treatment in the selection process. Back in the early 1970s, affirmative action was being implemented to the fullest extent by many colleges and universities. I support affirmative action, but I also know it has been abused by some universities.

I received a letter from MIT in the early spring of 1974, which said it received over two hundred applications and that the first round of the selection process had been completed. The letter further stated that only eighty applicants were selected for the next review and that I was one of them. I was more than excited because I knew at the time how hard it was to get admitted to MIT. The next letter informed me they admitted only twenty applicants for the fall session. I was very disappointed I was not one of the applicants admitted. However, I had not heard from UCLA yet, so there was still hope for entering graduate school. I felt somewhat depressed for a week after hearing from MIT.

While waiting for an answer from UCLA, I wondered at times whether identifying my race would have given me a better leverage for admission to the school. But I also felt that I did the right thing by not identifying my race. It was very important to me to be selected based on my academic record as well as my accomplishments outside of the academic world. Two weeks after I received my rejection letter from MIT, I received a letter from UCLA congratulating me for being selected to enter graduate school in the fall of 1974. My dream of entering graduate school for the fall had come true, and I thanked God for his blessings.

Prior to graduating from Cal State, both Lester and I were offered jobs in Boulder, Colorado. The jobs were at the same company that employed Lester after he resigned from D-Q University. It had received a federal government contract to perform some studies on the educational process and progress of Native-American schools located on Native-American land.

When I graduated from Cal State, Lester had completed the first year of his doctoral program. After my graduation ceremony, we started preparing for our move to Boulder for the summer. Casey and I were excited about living in a cool place for the summer. We wanted to go hiking and do some exploring in the mountains. While searching for an apartment the next day, we discovered that the university owned an apartment building near the university for their married students. We, of course, wanted to be near the campus as well as students since we were still part of the student environment. We found a daycare center that was rated number one in the community. We enrolled Casey, who was more than happy for me to enroll her at the daycare center because they told her they held classes in art and other drawing activities. She loved art and was an excellent artist.

Life in Boulder started out well. Casey was having fun at the daycare center, and we were deep into our work on the process and progress of Native-American education. On weekends, the three of us went on trips to the mountains and even went fishing high up in the Colorado Mountains. It was a wonderful summer until one noon at the end of July, when Lester got upset over a sandwich. He asked me if I would go to lunch with him, and with the sandwiches he picked up for us, I was to meet him at the picnic area near the building where other office workers also congregated during their lunch break.

I met him at the park and found that he did not pick up the type of sandwich I had requested. I told him so, but I would eat it anyway. Although I spoke calmly, he still got angry, which caused me to get angry with him. We ended up saying a few nasty words to each other, and I returned to the office without eating.

That afternoon, I made a decision to leave since my intuition told me that the small argument would give him an excuse to start disappearing from home for the remainder of the summer. I definitely did not want to go through the hardship I had experienced in the past. The emotional and physical abuses were beginning to destroy my self-worth.

Sure enough, at the end of the day he said he had to stay at the office and for me to pick up Casey and go home. I knew he would not come home, so I talked with Casey to let her know that we were going to visit her grandparents in New Mexico in the morning. She was excited since she loved the open space on their ranch. As I had suspected, Lester never came home that evening. Fortunately, I had the car so I was able to drive Casey to the daycare center in the morning. After letting the center know that this was Casey's last day and making arrangements to pick her up at noon, I went to the office. I informed the secretary that it was necessary for me to head back to Los Angeles to take care of some things at the university. I submitted my resignation that morning.

To this day, I don't know why the secretary said to me, "Women should never just walk away, washing diapers and caring for one's family is worth something." Her statement took me by surprise, so much so that I thought maybe she had psychic abilities and knew my life history. That day, I just wanted to leave and never look back. I felt old and tired before my time. My heart did lift knowing that I could care for my daughter with my scholarship and fellowship funds that had been recently awarded to me for graduate school. This one small summer incident finally broke the camel's back, so I thought at the time.

Casey and I spent the summer with my parents during the month of August. I never notified my husband of our destination at the time we left, nor did I contact him for the next two weeks. Casey, of course, kept asking for us to call her dad so she could talk to him. She could not understand why we could not call him. She kept saying, "I love Daddy and miss him. So can we call him?" I finally decided to call and let Casey talk to him. She was so excited she kept skipping around while talking to him. My heart broke in half knowing that one day she might have to grow up without him. After a lengthy conversation with her dad, he asked to talk to me.

He wanted to know what my plans were, and I said we were leaving for Los Angeles the last week of August and that I intended to start graduate work. He wanted to drive us back to Los Angeles, which was fine with me because I wanted Casey to spend some time with him. This was the beginning of the end.

Many people wonder why women choose to stay with their husbands when things go wrong in their marriage. I know from experience that when you have a child or children, it is very difficult to just think of your wellbeing. You always think of your children's happiness first, especially if they are at a very young age. I always thought of my daughter's happiness first, and that is why I worked so hard at keeping my marriage together. However, when the children notice there is much unhappiness in the home, it is time to let go. Children should never have to sacrifice their happiness when their parents no longer love or respect each other. They can sense an unhappy home life, and it will, in many cases, affect their lives.

## Chapter 11

In the evening of the last Thursday in August, we picked up Lester at the airport and spent time with my parents before leaving for Los Angeles on Saturday morning. Casey chatted with her dad most of the way back to Los Angeles. He told Casey and me that he was flying back to Boulder after he got us home since he was scheduled to fly to Washington, D.C. He said he was representing the company on a project it had completed and could not afford to miss the meeting. He also said he would be flying home to us in two weeks to continue his doctoral program.

I just assumed he would spend the night with us when we arrived home, but he did a shocker. As soon as he got the entire luggage unloaded and put in the apartment, he called a taxi and said he had an airline ticket to return to Boulder that evening. He did not even sit down for a minute. I still remember Casey, with tears in her eyes, saying, "Dad, please call me and Mom when you get back. I love you and I will miss you." I felt so sorry for Casey and decided at that moment I had to try harder to keep our family together.

Both Casey and I started school the second week of September—she, at the Catholic school located two blocks from home, and me, at UCLA, a thirty-minute drive from home. I had arranged my schedule so that I could take her to school and also pick her up. I was so happy to be attending graduate school, and all the negative happenings in my life seemed to disappear that first day on campus.

UCLA has a beautiful campus. Casey and I spent many hours either at the student library or on the lawn sitting on the benches located throughout the campus. I loved being on the grounds of UCLA and would miss it later on when I moved to D.C.

One week after I started school, Lester began his doctoral studies for his third and final year. He only had a couple of courses left to complete but still had the doctoral dissertation to complete. Since he did not have many courses to take, he did a lot of consulting work in Boulder for the organization that employed him during the summer months. His travels to Boulder for the consulting work were at least once a month and sometimes more. Casey and I did not see much of him that year because of the trips to Boulder and his periodic disappearances from home. I was so busy with my graduate studies that the arguments and his disappearing acts did not cause me much sadness or pain in my heart. I also no longer worried about him when he disappeared, like I did in the past.

One painful memory that sticks with me to this day took place in the spring of my first year in graduate school. Lester wanted to drive me to UCLA one morning so he could attend to some business on campus. He did not have classes that day, but I had classes until 3:00 P.M. that day. We arrived on campus and parked in our student-reserved parking space. The reserved section of the student parking lot was still empty of cars at that time of the morning. As we were getting out of the car, I asked for the car keys, but he said no and that he needed the car. I asked for the car keys again and told him I needed the car to pick up Casey at school at 4:00 P.M. I guess he expected me to take public transportation home and walk down to Casey's school and pick her up. I then asked if he could pick her up, and he said he could not because he wouldn't be home in time.

Anger rushed throughout my body, and I started walking away while yelling, "Keep the damn keys!" I made sure no one was around in the parking lot before I made the obscene remark. Next thing I knew, a ring of keys hit me in the neck. I was so stunned that at first I did not feel the pain. A few seconds later, the pain rushed to my head, and I stood there for a few minutes to make sure I did not faint. Fortunately, the heavy ring of keys did not cut me, but it did leave a big bruise. Within a few minutes, a large red welt appeared. I could not go to class sporting the latest assault from my husband, so I pushed up the collar on my sweater. True to form, my husband stayed away from home for several days after the incident. Later that day, I decided that hitting me with a ring of keys was just as bad as hitting me with his fist or shoving me around. I decided to tell him when he got home that I would not take any more abuse. I waited for a week after he returned home to discuss the key-hitting scenario in a calm and civil manner. I told him that hitting me with the keys would, indeed, be the last of any abuses from him, physical or emotional. He just sat there and smiled and said, "What about arguments?" to which I said that was okay, as long as they were civil. I said that arguments are considered normal in any marriage as long as they do not get out of hand. He sat there for a while and then said, "If that is the rule, it shall be the rule."

During the second semester of my first year of graduate work, one of my professors wanted me to take part in an internship program he had established with the university and the Department of Housing and Urban Development in Washington. I was to perform a public housing survey during the summer, but I was to be paid as soon as I signed the contract. The survey was to be performed on public housing built on the Navajo Indian Reservation in Window Rock, Arizona. I accepted the offer, signed the contract, and a check was provided to me that week.

I finished my first year of graduate work in very good standing. Lester also completed his course work in very good standing but had not completed his dissertation. He was not required to work on his dissertation on campus, so he decided to work on it at home. He wanted to do some consulting work that year as well. One evening the week after school ended, he discussed his plans for the coming year with me. Lester had been offered a job with one of the federal agencies in Washington, D.C. Evidently he received the job offer several weeks before school ended. But of course, he did not bother to tell me about the offer right away. Looking back, I believe he looked at all the alternatives that would benefit him and not the family before he told me about the job offer.

To my surprise, a miracle happened one evening. Lester, for once, wanted my input on two plans that he was thinking about. One plan was for him to stay with us in California and devote fifty percent of his time on completing his dissertation and fifty percent on doing consulting work for the company he worked for in Boulder. He said the consulting work would require him to spend one to two weeks in Boulder every other month. The other plan was to accept the job in Washington. He said that if he did accept the job, I could transfer to George Washington University and complete my graduate work there. I knew right at that moment I did not want to transfer to another school and delay my graduation. After a brief discussion, we both decided he should take the job in Washington. We also agreed that Casey and I should remain in Los Angeles so that I could finish my master's program.

I wanted to stay in California and finish school because transferring to another school, which would delay my graduation date possibly by one year. Also, the universities in the Washington Metropolitan area probably would not admit me that fall. Therefore, I would have to wait until the spring session to start school. I encouraged him to take the job in Washington because it sounded like it was a great opportunity that could not be passed up. I was truly happy for him, not only because of the excellent salary he was offered but also for the opportunity to work in our nation's policy-making center.

On the surface, I was happy for him, yet at the same time I wanted him to go so Casey and I could have some peace at home. I felt guilty for encouraging Lester to accept the job offer because deep in my heart, I wanted him to be out of my way in my last year of graduate work. I wanted to devote as much time as possible to studying and taking care of Casey. I still had some very difficult courses to complete, which required a voluminous amount of study time. I also wanted a less stressful life for Casey and me during my last year of graduate school.

Lester and I planned to search and purchase a car for me prior to us leaving for our separate destinations. I not only needed a car to perform the survey that summer, but for both Casey and me in the coming school year. A week before we left Los Angeles, I searched around the San Fernando Valley for car dealerships that offered sales on new cars. I wanted a small car that did not use too much gas, and the only luxury that I wanted to be included in the car was an air conditioner. I found a dealership in Canoga Park, California, which was about twenty miles from home. The local newspaper indicated they had plenty of cars of various makes and models on sale.

Lester went with me to check out the cars, but he was not very helpful. He kept selecting cars that were larger and less economical than what I wanted. I stuck to my plan of getting a small and economical car even though he kept pressuring me to get something bigger. Yes, I found exactly what I wanted, and it was a small 1975 Toyota Corolla four-door FWD sedan. It had only the basic features but included an air conditioner at no extra cost. Back in the 1970s, air conditioners were considered luxury items and were not part of the basic features as today. This was my first car, so I was excited like a high school girl. I was even more excited when I realized that the price was within my reach. Cars, especially Toyotas, were inexpensive in those days. I was able to pay for it with the money I saved from previous summer jobs.

## Chapter 12

As done in the past, we paid our rent for the apartment for the summer months and left all our household items in the house. Again, the same female landlord who watched our apartment the previous summer said she would keep an eye on the place. She offered, and we accepted, that she would go into the apartment periodically to make sure everything was fine. She knew that Casey and I would be returning in the fall and that Lester would be located in Washington.

We left on an early Saturday morning in two cars. Lester was to spend a day or two with us in Window Rock, where I was to report for my internship before he went on to Washington. Lester drove his car and I drove my new car with Casey. I stayed behind him on the freeway out of Los Angeles but lost him on the outskirts of the city, where the freeway splits into two highways. Both of these highways went east. I was not sure which highway he took, so I made a quick decision to take the one that turned to the right, not knowing he had taken the one to the left.

Casey and I kept traveling, hoping to catch up with her dad, but it appeared hopeless after a couple of hours. I did not want to turn around and go back to the other highway out of Los Angeles, so I just kept driving. Around noon, I looked at a map at a gas station and found out that I could get back to the main highway going east if I took the next two-lane highway going north. The highway going north was rough going. A desolate and scary area, I was glad for my new car. Hopefully, it would at least stay the course and not break down. A flat tire or an accident in a place like this would be far from ideal. A woman on her own with a small child for company would be at the mercy of strangers. I shuddered to think and kept going. In those days, there were no cell phones to call for help or GPSs to help locate one's position anywhere on the planet.

Thankfully, we made it to the main highway without striking one of the potholes and ending up stranded alongside the road, but it was getting dark, so I decided it best to find a motel and check in for the evening.

After a little searching, we located one in a small town situated off one of the exits. After checking in, I informed the desk clerk that my husband, who was driving another car, had got separated from me and requested he call me from the front desk should my husband show up later in the evening. While Casey explored some of the flyers in the lobby of the motel, I called my sister in Window Rock, where I was to execute the housing survey that summer. After some haggling with the operator for my sister's unlisted number, I managed to place a collect call. To my relief, she accepted and the operator let me through to her. I explained what had happened, and she replied that Lester had already contacted her and would call again later in the hopes that by then my sister would know where we were. I gave her the address and she promised to pass it on to him. At around midnight, Lester finally arrived at the motel. After contacting my sister, he had driven back toward the motel, backtracking his journey. Apparently, when we took the secondary highway that morning, he had taken the main one going east.

By the time we arrived at Window Rock, the owner of the small house I was to rent had already leased it to a petroleum engineer, who was hired to assist the tribe on some other projects. Frustrated, I was faced with a rather long commute from outlying areas such as Gallup or Farmington, New Mexico. Thanks to my sister, we managed to find a room in a home where the owner was visiting her children out of state for the summer. As planned, Lester departed for Washington, D.C., after a couple of days with Casey and me. Lester called us once a week to make sure all our activities were going well in Arizona. Casey loved talking to her dad and always looked forward to his weekly calls. Two weeks after he arrived in Washington, he called one evening to say he was lonely and wanted Casey and me to move to Washington. Even though Casey and I spent most of the time alone since her birth, we were also lonely living in Arizona. He wanted me to quit the project, return the internship money to UCLA, which was still in my savings account, and transfer to one of the universities in Washington, D.C.

I gave some serious thought to going to Washington, but only because Casey missed her dad so much. After some thought, I decided uprooting to D.C. would mean a disruption to my degree, and by now I was finished with succumbing to Lester's wishes. After all, what might we be moving to? The move could result in nights alone while he went off on one of his night or weeklong absences. What he missed was my convenience to him, someone to clean and cook for, to be there when he felt like it. Right now, Casey and I had a calm home, a sense of peace I was not willing to part with.

We met only on one occasion during the summer. He flew into Albuquerque for a business meeting. Casey and I drove for two hours to meet him for dinner. It was lovely to see her so excited to finally get to spend time with her father. I remember we had a wonderful weekend. We spent shopping for Casey's school clothes while her father attended the meeting that Saturday morning. In the evening we met up again, then after breakfast Sunday morning, Lester returned to D.C.

## The Forgotten American

I was busy all summer. Selected via a random sampling technique administered by my former professor at UCLA, I was to interview the head of every household within the survey sample. Most were cooperative, but some were rude. Even once explained I was a member of the Navajo Tribe, they viewed me with skepticism. There were times, though, when my efforts were rewarded once I explained the survey was to benefit housing for the Navajo people.

Casey loved the open space on the Navajo Reservation and the Navajo food that we sometimes ate at one of the local restaurants. One of her favorite foods was Navajo taco. Fry bread is the base of a Navajo taco, which is topped with ground beef, tomatoes, cheese, onions, and lettuce. Fry bread is flat dough fried in oil similar to a flour tortilla but much thicker. The bread is called "fry bread" and not "fried bread."

## Chapter 13

As soon as I completed the survey, I started making plans to return to Los Angeles. Casey and I were very happy to find out that her dad had a business trip to Farmington the last week of August. He had made plans to meet us in Farmington and drive us back to Los Angeles. We packed our things and drove to Farmington on a Thursday and checked into the hotel Lester had reserved for us. That evening he called to tell us his meeting scheduled for Friday was cancelled and for us to meet him Friday evening in Gallup, one hundred twenty-one miles away.

Since we were not scheduled to meet Lester until Friday evening, Casey and I visited several relatives in the area. During our visit, Casey told everyone that her dad was working in Washington, D.C., and her mother was going to finish school in Los Angeles that year. I will never forget one statement she made and to this day, my heart breaks into pieces when I think of it. She said, "I will miss my dad so much."

We met on Friday evening, and Casey was so excited to see her dad. We all had a wonderful time on the trip back to Los Angeles. Lester stayed with us for a couple of days. When we took him to the airport for Washington, Casey cried at the airport and on the way home. I assured her that he loved her and that he would call her every week.

School started the first week of September for both Casey and me. She started her third year, and I started my second and final year of graduate school. It was great to be back on the UCLA campus with young students from many different parts of the United States and foreign countries—all eager to get an education and some to party. Casey and I spent many weekends on campus that school year. While I studied, she would write stories or read books. We often went to the campus eatery to eat sweet crepes for lunch. Sometimes we would get an ice cream cone in the afternoon.

Lester was good about calling every week for the first two months but tapered off the following months. I tried to call him many times at his apartment in the evenings, but the phone just rang off the hook. He always said he was working late or was working on his dissertation at the library. There were no answering machines in those days, so I could not leave a message on his telephone to call me. Because I was so busy with my studies and taking care of Casey, I did not question him. Looking back to those days, I now know that he never worked on his dissertation or worked late at the office. By this time, he had become such a good liar that he probably began to believe his own lies.

In November, Lester managed to swing a trip to visit Casey and me in Los Angeles via a business trip to San Diego. For Casey's sake, I was so glad the trip coincided with the Thanksgiving holiday. It was wonderful watching her relay stories to her father concerning her various escapades at school. A natural at drawing, she had been selected to draw Thanksgiving artwork for the classroom window that year, and she was so proud telling her father all about this.

Around noon on Thanksgiving Day, the telephone rang, and I answered it, but there was no one at the other end so I hung up. Within a few minutes, it rang again, and I answered and a woman asked to speak to Lester. I could hear some giggling in the background. He spoke briefly to the woman and when he hung up the phone, I asked who called. He said it was one of the secretaries confirming his return flight to Washington. I was not suspicious but should have been. Thinking back to that time, I now believe that my husband was having a great time with a slutty woman and not working at the office late or the library as he had been telling me all along.

The afternoon of Lester's departure, I became very ill. Casey accompanied me to the emergency room and after waiting several hours; the doctors who finally examined me were unable to determine the cause of my illness. They asked if my husband had been to Mexico recently and perhaps transferred the illness to me. I told then several of his colleagues had, but not him as far as I was aware.

I never did manage to find out what caused the mysterious illness. The doctors were not able to provide answers, either. Later that night, when I arrived back at the apartment, I contacted Lester and of course, he was none the wiser, either. Where Lester was concerned, I had come to realize, there never would be a straight answer.

## Chapter 14

Lester wanted Casey and me to go to Washington for our Christmas break instead of him coming to California. Casey and I were to fly to Washington on Friday morning, and we were so excited that we hardly slept on Thursday night. Our flight arrived in the late afternoon, and Lester was waiting for us at the gate. After having lunch, my husband took us to a Christmas party in the federal building where he worked. Everyone was having a great time, and the Christmas decorations were beautiful. We met many people, young and old, who all said they had been waiting to meet us. A few people told us they thought we really did not exist and that Lester had dreamed up a family for himself.

About a week after we arrived, Casey got very sick. Her temperature kept rising, so we took her to the doctor, who said she had the flu. I did not do much that week since Casey was ill. I was neither annoyed nor suspicious when Lester came home really late at night several times while we were visiting him. I was more concerned about my dear Casey being sick. His excuse for coming home late was that he had a lot of work that had to be completed before the start of business the next day. He said he could not break away sooner. One evening he received a call, and after a brief moment of silence, he said, "My family is in town." He went on to tell the person at the other end that he couldn't talk and would call back in the morning. I thought I saw a look of guilt when he hung up the phone but didn't bother to ask who called.

Casey recovered from her illness before New Year's Eve, so Lester planned for us to attend a party at the Crystal Gateway Marriott Hotel in Rosslyn, Virginia. Because I did not like leaving Casey with babysitters, he reserved a room for us at the hotel so Casey could watch television while we attended the New Year's party. We also wanted to check on her periodically during the party to make sure she was safe and happy. Both Lester and I had a good time, but it was rather strange that he kept disappearing for short periods of time. When I asked him where he went or what he was up to, he would say that he went to the men's room or that he went to say hello to someone at the bar. Here was another sign that the long-distance marriage was beginning to fall apart, but I did not have a clue as to what was happening.

The last evening we spent in Washington was not a happy one. Lester did not return home until after 9:00 P.M., and by then, Casey was asleep. I called his office a dozen times that evening, but no one was there to answer the phone. At one point, I was afraid he had gotten killed while walking to the parking lot. By the time he arrived home, I was so angry that I hardly spoke to him. I certainly did not want to hear his poor excuses for not calling us to let us know his whereabouts. He said he and several of his colleagues went to the lounge at the Marriott Hotel to have a few drinks, and time flew away from him. I wanted to believe him, but there was much doubt in my mind. However, at the same time, I could not imagine any woman wanting to have a tryst with him.

The next morning, I called a taxicab to go to the airport since I did not want to be around him anymore. But he insisted that he drive us to the airport so he could see us off. He said he was going to miss us very much. Casey, of course, wanted to be with her dad and was more than happy to have him see us off. For her sake, I agreed but said very little to him on the way to and at the airport. As we flew away, something told me that we would not hear from him very often from that day forward, which was exactly what, happened.

In the New Year, I decided to enroll Casey in a local ballet class. Since the age of four, she had been imitating ballet steps, so I thought it might be a good idea. Susan, her teacher, was strict, as all good ballet teachers are. Well liked by her students, including Casey, she was considered one of the best ballet teachers in the area. Spring came and went in a blur of activity. Between my studies and Casey's ballet classes and at-home practices, she scarcely noticed that her father never called. Nevertheless, she was looking forward to spending time with him in the summer.

One incident during that spring has stuck with me over the years. Shortly before Mother's Day, Lester called to ask what I wanted as a present. Apparently, he wanted to purchase something nice for me. After telling him I would love a ring set with my birthstone, he told me it would arrive before the special day. Of course, it didn't show up, I should have known better than to get my hopes up. Angry, I called him for one week afterward as late as 1:00 A.M. his time but could not find him at home.

Eventually, I managed to get in touch with him one morning at his office. Although he apologized for not being in touch, he could not offer any explanation for it. After saying he would make more of an effort to stay in touch, he promised to send the ring. At this point, I couldn't care less about the ring. I was more concerned about the lies I knew he was feeding me.

I graduated that June with my master's degree in city and regional planning.

## The Forgotten American

The weather was beautiful that day, no "June Bloom" dull weather in L.A. that day. Everyone smiled on campus, I guess looking forward to the summer vacations and family get-togethers to come.

Driving home, I realized there was still a long road ahead in order for me to be fully self- sufficient, and I had no idea what was ahead of me with regard to my marriage. Unbelievably, despite an uneasy feeling of dread ahead of me, I was excited about moving east and meeting the challenges of finding work in D.C. Excited about being with her dad again, Casey could talk of nothing other than him flying to L.A. the following week, from which he would drive us back east.

## Chapter 15

We had a great time driving back east. Casey chatting with her father, excited to be seeing him every day. I even began to believe everything was going to be okay. This was a fresh start for all of us. We could be together and be a normal family like everyone else. I began to grow hopeful, too. After living in Lester's leased apartment for a short period, we managed to locate a nice townhome in a newly developed suburb in northern Virginia. We were to purchase new furniture together, as we had donated all our old furniture to Goodwill. Casey was enrolled in a private Catholic school with an excellent curriculum and seemed happy to continue with her education in a new school. After we settled in our new home, all appeared to be fine for the first week, and then Lester started coming home late in the evenings. I knew that most employees who work for the federal government normally stop for the day around 5:00 or 6:00 P.M., and I often wondered why he was returning home so late. I would dismiss any negative thoughts that crept into my head and convince myself that he had a lot of work. After all, he was a special assistant to one of the commissioners in the agency. After one month of coming home late, Lester failed to come home at all one Friday night. I was very worried but could not call or do anything since I did not know the area too well yet. He finally came home around 9:00 A.M. on the next day and was happy as a lark. Casey and I were outside playing with a white cat that often came to visit us in our backyard. He was a stray cat that the neighborhood children named Snowball.

Lester wanted us to go to New York for the weekend but never explained where he had been all night. We arrived in New York City Saturday evening and went on several guided tours all day Sunday. We had a good time but when we started home on Monday morning, I sensed something terrible was going on in Lester's life.

Shortly after our trip to New York City, Lester again went missing on a Friday night. When he arrived home on a Saturday morning, he wanted us to go on a picnic that day. I guess this was his way of trying to erase his guilt for not coming home that night. The day turned out to be a very good day for Casey and me.

One bright spot was Snowball, confirmed as a stray cat by the neighbors; Casey was determined to adopt him, even against her father's wishes. The animal had survived a harsh Virginia winter by sleeping under cars and dining on whatever table scraps the neighborhood children could sneak from their houses. So after several weeks of vet checkups and shots, the little cat was given a home. Snowball gave Casey many hours of love and play. He always knew when she was coming home from school, and he would wait at the front door for her. As soon as she walked in, he would jump on her knees and paw at them while she stood at the door. When she went out to play with the children, he also wanted to go, and I would let him out. However, within a few minutes, Casey would bring him back and tell me that he had to stay in the house because the neighborhood boys were out and could get rough with him. Snowball did not like being inside when Casey played outside. He would drive me crazy with his constant loud meows while standing at the kitchen window with his paws on the windowsill. The neighbors across the street told me one evening they could see Snowball at the window meowing quite often and thought it was very cute.

Looking for employment was not an easy task, especially with little employment history behind me. I was determined to get a job with the federal government, but I knew I had to get a job that did not require me to travel or require long-term training, which would take me away from Casey. Shortly after we settled into our new home, during the latter part of June 1976, I started applying for jobs. Since computers were not yet available, I could not search for job vacancies as it can be done today. It was hard looking for a job. I was pretty discouraged by November of that year, since not one agency or private organization had responded to my applications. Friday evening in October, four months after Casey and I had moved to Washington, Lester brought home a brand-new car. Pontiac called the model Trans Am. He said the salesman let him take it home overnight on a trial basis. He said he needed a new car that had more horsepower and his car was beginning to have problems. He seemed to be very distant that evening, and sad. I felt badly for him, believing it was work related.

The next day, he got up very early and worked in his office at home all day. Around 4:00 P.M., he asked Casey and me to go to the car dealership with him. He said he made a decision to purchase the car. While we were there, I offered to give him one thousand dollars to use as an additional down payment. I told him I had two thousand dollars that I had saved over the years. The reason I offered the money was because I felt sorry for him, thinking his job was getting him down. He accepted the offer, and I wrote him a check right there at the dealership. I must have been out of my mind to offer that kind of money when I had no job. My advice to women who are facing what I endured years ago is: "Hang on to every penny you save because you may need it for you and your children in an emergency." I deeply regret making such a foolish decision because I did need the money later that year.

## Chapter 16

Thanksgiving and Christmas were very unhappy times for both Casey and me. We were invited to Thanksgiving dinner at one of Lester's colleague's homes. The family had three children who were a little older than Casey but young enough to entertain her with games that day. The wife of the colleague was an excellent cook, and she cooked a fabulous dinner.

After a wonderful Thanksgiving dinner, we left for home, and by then it was dark outside. As soon as we got in the house, Lester said he had to go to the 7-Eleven store to get some things but did not say exactly what he needed. It took him thirty minutes to return home, and I asked what he purchased and why it took so long. He said the store was out of the type of headache pills he preferred and he got carried away talking to the night manager. Today, I know he went to the 7-Eleven store near home to call someone from the pay phone. He evidently did not want me to hear his conversation. There were no cell phones in those days, so the only way he could call whomever he wanted to call was through a pay telephone.

Lester continued to come home very late or not at all through the month of December. I started suspecting that he was having an affair with some slutty type of woman. So I started looking through his clothes in the dirty clothes hamper every week but did not find anything that was suspicious during the first month of my search. By this time, I rarely spoke to him even though we were still sleeping in the same bed. Since he would come home around midnight, there was no reason to start a conversation with him. He usually left before Casey and I got up for the day, so there was even less reason to talk to him. I knew Casey could feel my sadness and anger even though I tried to keep on a happy face. She also could see that her dad was never home, not only during the week but also on Saturdays and, at times, the whole weekend.

After we got settled in Virginia, I made sure that Casey continued her ballet lessons, so I enrolled her in one of the schools close to home. I would drive her to ballet lessons after school on Wednesdays, and I would go to the restaurant next door until she finished her lessons. I usually had a cup of coffee or tea and sometimes a glass of wine at the restaurant to relax and plan our future without her dad. The future I was planning for us had to be modest. I knew I would not have much money even after I landed a job since entry-level jobs normally had low salaries. Therefore, it was absolutely necessary to plan modestly.

Just before Christmas, I did my Christmas shopping for the family, including Lester. However, this cruel, deceitful man did not even have the decency to shop for Casey or me. Two days before Christmas, he did not bother to come home and was missing in action through New Year's Day. Despite my husband's emotional abuse, I telephoned one of his colleagues on Christmas Day. I kept imagining that he was either dead somewhere in Washington, D.C., or in the hospital with injuries. Unfortunately, the colleague had no idea where he had gone and said it did not sound like him. Little did he know that this man was not only a horrible husband but also a totally useless dad to Casey.

The colleague called me later that afternoon to find out if I knew how to cook a goose and also to find out if Lester had returned home. Having never cooked a goose, I told him I could not help but if he had a cookbook I could guide him through the preparation process on the telephone. This man was a single parent and between the two of us, we figured out the cooking method, and he thanked me many times before hanging up the telephone.

After that telephone call, I decided not to worry or care about Lester anymore. Casey and I cooked a small turkey and had Christmas dinner by ourselves. My immediate family was far away, and I had only a couple of woman friends who had their own families to tend to that day. I am a very private person, so no one knew the problems I had in my marriage. I had no one to talk to about my problems, not even my own family, who probably could not offer any advice anyway. My mother, happily married her whole life, did not believe in divorce. My parents had stayed married until the death of my mother. Since the incident with the professor's wife years earlier, I trusted no one. Embarrassed and distrustful, I kept everything to myself.

Casey and I spent Christmas and New Year's Day alone, but we had a pretty good time. We baked some cookies and played games and camped in the living room, which Casey loved to do. We also made sure that Snowball had a good time, so we played hide-and-seek with him in the woods behind our house. Snowball was a very smart cat that always found our hiding places within a few minutes.

Lester eventually returned home around midnight the following day after New Year's Day. He never bothered to say, "Happy New Year," to either Casey or me. He also did not bring any presents for Casey. I figured he would not bother to get me anything but had hoped he had some kindness in his heart to get a nice gift for Casey. I felt so badly for Casey, but she did not appear to be sad or angry that he had no Christmas presents for her. I think, by this time, she realized he was not such a great dad as she had thought in the past. She no longer asked about him in the evenings or weekends when he failed to return home. In fact, she seemed to be happier when he was not at home.

A month after Christmas, while paying a credit card bill, I saw a charge for a very large amount to one jewelry store near our home. I visited the store later that day and found out the purchase of a ring was from the very expensive section of the women's jewelry department. Since I did not get anything for Christmas from Lester, I knew something horrible was going on behind my back. After getting all the information, I heard the store associate asking me if I was all right. I was not all right but said I was fine and left the store with tears running down my face. The purchase of an expensive jewelry, coupled with the lack of Christmas presents for Casey and me, meant only one thing. He had a mistress. I cried for days, my suspicious confirmed. Knowing nothing of this, Casey went to school, oblivious. I could not bear for her to see me upset, so I kept the tears to myself.

## Chapter 17

I continued searching Lester's clothes to see if I could find anything that would shed light on his long absences from home. One Monday morning in March, as I was preparing his clothes to take to the dry cleaners, I found a note in one of his trouser pockets. The note said: "I love you and need you every day. Love, Jane." The note was on plain yellow-lined writing paper. I was so shocked that I stood there for a long time trying to comprehend the message. I finally came to my senses and went to the bedroom and sat down on the bed. I sat there for a long time, and I could see myself in the bedroom dresser mirror located across from the bed. My face had turned pale, and my eyes were wide with fright. I was so shocked that I could not even cry.

After sitting like a zombie for almost thirty minutes, I finally came to my full senses. Tears streamed down my face, and I wondered if the note had been deliberately left, knowing I would find it. I wanted to find the woman who wrote the note. I hated her. I needed to see her. After crying everything out, I completed some chores, before reserving the afternoon to search for this woman by contacting the few people I knew in the D.C. area.

The first call was to my friend Marcey, who worked at the federal agency where Lester was employed. I called her to see if she knew a woman by the name of Jane. Since I was not yet ready to tell anyone of my findings, I told her I received a call from a woman who had gone to a reception the previous evening in D.C. She had met a Native-American woman by the name of Jane but forgot her last name. Marcey said she did not know any Native-American woman named Jane but would check within the organization where she worked. It did not take her long to find out there was indeed a woman by that name who worked as a secretary for a Native-American organization in Washington. She gave me the full name of the woman, as well as the name and telephone number of the Native-American organization where this woman worked. I was elated that my investigation was successful but also scared and nervous about taking the next step. I knew that Lester would abuse me either physically or emotionally once he found out I was snooping around, but I couldn't care less. He had betrayed me.

The next morning, while Casey was at school, I headed to D.C. and parked at the building where the woman worked. Trembling from a mix of anger and fear, I swallowed the lump in my throat and concentrated on locating the floor where this woman worked. Heart pounding, I stepped off the elevator, determined to follow through on my mission. I wanted to know what she looked like, needed to understand the relationship she had with my husband.

Entering the office, I observed a young woman somewhere in her late twenties sitting outside another office with the title "Director" on top of the door. Heavyset with long hair and not very attractive, I assumed from where she sat to be the secretary to the organization. She asked if she could help me and after I introduced myself, she inhaled sharply and turned red.

I told her I wanted to talk to her about her relationship with Lester, my husband. She immediately got up from the desk and pointed to the empty desk to her left, which was located closer to the entrance. This desk probably belonged to a clerk who fortunately, for her, was not present at the time. I assumed we moved to that desk because she did not want her boss to hear the conversation. She sat in the clerk's chair, and I sat down in the chair in front of the desk. I immediately told her I had found a note signed by her in one of my husband's trouser pockets. I also held up the note where she could clearly see it. She began to sweat and said that she and my husband were only friends. I told her that I did not believe her and told her to get my husband on the phone for proof. I noticed she was able to dial his number without looking it up in a telephone book or office directory.

He must have answered on the first ring because she immediately said she needed to talk to him. She sounded nervous, and her voice was quivering when she told him that his wife was in her office. He must have asked her to put me on the phone since she handed it to me. I took it, and Lester said to me that I should not be bothering people at work and should go home. I quickly said I wanted some answers on their relationship. I also told him about finding the note signed by Jane in one of his trousers the day before. I offered to read the note to him but he requested, in almost a begging tone, that I not read it. He said that Jane and he were just friends and that he would explain everything to me that evening.

I knew the information about them being just friends was a big fat lie. I hung up the telephone, got up, and said to her that everything they said was a lie. I walked out and knew in my heart that he would continue his relationship with the slut. I felt very sad, not so much for me but for my beautiful lovely daughter, Casey. I could not believe that Lester would be having an affair with a secretary—and not a very attractive one, either.

Later I was told the secretary was known to have slept with many men in the area, but I did not bother to find out whether it was true or not. The question that

## The Forgotten American

was floating in my mind as I left was: "Why do some successful men destroy their marriages for secretaries who are often not very attractive?" As one woman TV news reporter said one evening: "Why do men always cheat down?" Asked what she meant by that, her response was: "Many men usually have affairs with women who are less attractive and less educated than their wives."

On the way home, I tried to cry to ease my pain but could not even cry. I knew I was at a great disadvantage since I had little money and still had no job. However, I decided it was time to start some serious planning for a different kind of life without Lester. I went home that day and called Steve, an acquaintance whom both Lester and I had known for some time. I was so distressed that I needed to talk to someone, and I selected him because he frequently had lunch with Lester. I wanted to see if he knew anything about Lester and his mistress and if he knew how long it had been going on. I briefly discussed my findings and wanted to know if he and others knew that Lester was having an affair with some slutty secretary. He sounded shocked and assured me that he knew nothing about it and that he doubted if anyone else knew about the affair.

After giving more detailed information about my finding, Steve asked if I could come down to his office in Washington so we could talk some more. I told him I really did not think it was necessary for me to come to his office, but he insisted that it would be good for me talk about it with a friend. I finally agreed to meet him since I really needed to talk to someone I knew and who also knew Lester pretty well. Before driving to D.C., I asked the teenager next door to babysit Casey for a couple of hours, and she happily agreed.

Traffic was light headed back into D.C., and I was there in thirty minutes. He asked me to tell him the full story of my findings. I told him about some of the things I had experienced within the previous two months. I asked Steve why he did not know anything about the affair since he got together with Lester for lunch quite often. He said he truly did not know anything was going on because Lester would talk about Casey and me all the time. What a joke on him. He said on several occasions he asked Lester to have us come over for dinner, but Lester always turned down the invitation. He said he should have sensed things were not going too well for us when the dinner invitations were never accepted. After our talk, I took Steve back to his house, which was about six miles from our home. I did not ask him to keep the information and our talk a secret. I knew he would be on the phone to various people that evening, but I no longer cared who knew of the affair. For once I was glad I was not working and still at home, where no one could look at me with pity and maybe even joy.

Lester came home rather early the day I visited his mistress, Jane. I was sitting on the couch in the living room. He went directly upstairs and changed his clothes; when he came back down, he tore into me, saying, "You should not be bothering people at the office." I immediately said I wanted to meet his mistress, the secretary, and get the full story on his affair. He looked stunned that I would make such a comment. He insisted she was only a friend and that his coming home late was because of all the work he had to do each day. I saw no need to hear the lies or discuss the issue, so I got up and went upstairs to Casey's room, where she was doing her homework. We stayed in her room until he left, probably to go see his mistress. I was sure he would continue to come home late at night, if and when he did, to be with his slutty mistress.

The next morning, I called Marcey at her office and told her of the affair Lester was having, and she could not believe it. She said she ran into him at least once a week and would ask about Casey and me. She said he always said we were both fine and that he was happy to have us here in Washington.

That evening she came over with a bottle of wine to try to comfort me. Her company, along with the wine, did indeed do me some good. She told me that many people within the federal agency where she and Lester worked were just beginning to talk about the affair he was having. I told her I needed to find a job really soon because I could no longer stand being around him. I told her I was not having much luck and that I probably needed to do more than send resumes and follow-up letters. She agreed and suggested I call the human resources office in some of the agencies to find out if they received my resume. She also suggested that I visit some of the agencies and pick up their vacancy announcements. She assured me that a job was around the corner for me.

Shortly after I found out about the affair, I sat down with Casey and told her the complete story. I even told her the name of the woman, including the name and address of the organization where she worked. I wanted her to know the reason I wanted us to move to a new location and also in case anything ever happened to me before we moved away. I also assured her that her dad loved her and that he would always love her. I don't think she believed me. I wanted to keep all the doors open between her and her dad, no matter how I felt.

Several weeks after telling Casey about her dad's affair, I told her that I was planning on moving us to a new location as soon as I got a job. I told her it would have to be a small apartment since my salary most likely would not match her dad's salary. I also told her that many apartments did not accept cats but I would try to find one where the building management accepted cats. She said she wanted to move away so we could be happy again. We sat in her room crying and all of sudden, Snowball came running and jumped on the bed between us and started purring, which caused us to start laughing. It was as if someone struck us with a magic wand full of happiness. We knew then that whatever path we took everything would turn out fine.

Prior to public knowledge of his affair, Lester was very well respected and viewed as a kind, intelligent, and wise man. He was intelligent, but I would not consider him to be kind or wise. I also do not understand why he was respected. A wise man is someone like my grandfather, who was a kind, strong Indian tribal leader who protected and took care of his family. My grandfather fought for the rights of his people, and his leadership provided new opportunities for them. As a child, I remember him giving away bushels of corn to people in the community just before winter. On occasion, he would have the hired hands slaughter several cows to give to the less fortunate in his community so they could have food for the winter. That to me was a kind, wise man. A man who abuses his family and puts himself first before everyone else is certainly not a kind and wise man and does not deserve to be respected.

For the next few months, during the day while Casey was at school, I searched vigorously for a job while at the same time investigating Lester's nightly activities. I had planned to complete several missions within the next few weeks. The first mission was to find out if he was picking up his mistress every day after work, so I made a couple of trips to Washington. I made sure they did not see me, so I parked in the garage next door to where the mistress worked. I could see all the people who left the building from the garage where I was parked. I did not see her leave the first time I made the trip, but on my second trip, I saw him pull up at the end of the block, and she got into the car. So I now had evidence that they indeed were still having their sleazy affair.

My second mission was to find out where the mistress lived. I predicted that she lived in Virginia and probably somewhere near us. The area I selected for my search was near our home but too large to do a search in a reasonable period of time. So I decided to use the monthly credit card statements as my investigation tool. So for the next couple of months, I examined the statements and got lucky one morning. One credit card statement had a couple of gas stations listed, and another had an inexpensive department store that sells everything from tires to clothes.

I called the credit card company and told them I did not recognize the purchases, and I asked if they could look up the address where the purchases were made. Purchases on both statements were made at the department store on Edsall Road, which was near our home. The next thing I did was to write to the home office of the store and request a copy of the receipt for the purchase listed on the credit card statement. They charged me five dollars for the receipt I wanted, but it was worth the cost. When I received copies of the receipt, it showed the items purchased, the date of the purchases, and Lester's signature. The items he purchased were undershorts for men. It looked like he ran out of clean shorts and probably during the times he failed to come home. Based on my findings, I knew the mistress had to live near our home.

My third mission was to catch Lester going into or coming out of the apartment where his mistress lived. It had to be an apartment since she could not purchase a home on a secretary's salary. I started scouting around in my car after Casey left for school. I scouted around midmorning, when most employed people were at work and traffic was light. I found an apartment complex that did not look too expensive and decided to start my investigation there. My investigation around the large apartment complex was a little harder to do since I was not sure where to start my search. I got lucky on my third scouting trip. When he did not come home for several nights in the spring of that year, I decided to search around the apartment I had selected a third time. So I left early Saturday morning and searched for Lester's car in all of the parking lots of the apartment complex. I found his car parked near one building, so I parked nearby and went into one of the apartment buildings and looked at the directory.

The apartment directory did not list the name of the mistress, but my intuition said she had to live in that building, so I waited for a few minutes. I proceeded to knock on all three doors on the first level. Since no one came to these doors, I went back to my car and waited to see if Lester would come out of the building. Lo and behold, he came out of the building and as soon as he got in his car, I started my car and started following him out of the parking lot. Halfway home, he saw me and gunned his car, so I had to do the same thing, but fortunately he slowed down near our home. When we were both inside, I said to him that I had done some investigating and told him the results of my three missions and my findings. The only thing he could say was: "I guess the handwriting is on the wall." I did not even look at him or respond to his stupid comment and went upstairs to get Casey. She was ready to go as I had asked her to do before I left for my third mission.

## Chapter 18

Casey and I left for the day to look for an apartment, which had to be near her school and also where her school bus stopped to pick up the children. We found a new complex that was not too expensive and not too far from her school and the school bus stop. We went to the rental office to talk with the manager. She said they had a lot of vacancies in the new building since it had just been constructed. She believed there would be more vacancies in the next several months. I left my name as an interested occupant and gave them an approximate time when I would be contacting her again.

We were so happy we found a new building with good tenants who were near her school, the school bus stop, and a very nice grocery store. We went to lunch at a place called Ribsters and had hamburgers and fries, our favorite food to this day. The apartment we found could not take cats or dogs, so we discussed the future for Snowball. I told Casey that we could take him to the animal shelter, where he would most likely be adopted. She did not want him to be taken to the shelter, and I told her the other alternative was to have him euthanized by his veterinarian. She decided to have Snowball put to sleep because she did not want him to suffer in any way after we moved. I was so sad to hear my daughter say she wanted to have Snowball put down, but I wanted to do what she desired. I cried so hard that evening for Casey and Snowball and prayed for strength and guidance. My beautiful and precious child, Casey, was only eight years old but going on eighteen years mentally. She was very mature at that age and appeared to handle any crisis that developed in our lives. After she made her decision, we talked about all the joy and happiness that Snowball gave us. We made a promise to play with Snowball and to show him love every minute from that day until we took him to the veterinarian, and we did.

Around the middle of May, I was invited to a reception at the Russell Building on Capitol Hill in D.C. I called Lester and told him to stay home with Casey on a

Wednesday evening so I could go to a reception. The evening of the reception, he called to say he was just leaving the office and that I could leave since he believed Casey would be okay until he got home. I was not about to leave her alone, so I asked the teenage girl next door to stay with her until her dad came home within the next thirty minutes. She gladly accepted the sitting job since I was going to double her sitting service fee that evening.

I drove to the reception. The food was great, and I met many wonderful professional men and women. One of the women I talked to learned I had recently obtained my master's degree and was searching for employment. I told her that I had some work experience and the most recent experience was performing a survey on Native-American public housing. Based on the information I gave her, she said I might try the Department of Housing and Urban Development (HUD). This agency already had my resume, but I had never received any response. I decided right there and then to telephone the agency the next day to find out what happened to my resume.

The time spent at the reception gave me a boost on my outlook on life, and I left for home with a light and happy heart that evening. When I got home, it was around 10:00 P.M., and I could see that my bedroom light was still on. I was surprised to find the screen door locked since Lester knew I would be coming home around that time. The screen door had no lock to open from the outside, so I rang the doorbell several times. When it looked like no one was going to answer the door, I started calling Lester while knocking on the screen door. I heard someone running down the stairs and when the door opened, Lester had a gun in his hand and right behind him was Casey, who yelled out, "Mom, you're home!" Lester looked rather surprised that Casey had followed him.

After going upstairs and putting Casey to bed, I asked Lester why he came to the door with a gun since he knew I would be coming home around this time. He said, "You never know who is going to be at the door." I found this to be very disturbing and later that night; I wondered if he would have shot me if Casey had not followed him. I also wondered if he wanted me dead so he could be with his mistress. It might have been the mistress who wanted me out of the way and was putting pressure on him to leave his family. Little did they know that I was planning to leave that entire sleazy environment behind as soon as I found a job.

The reason I thought she was putting pressure on him to leave was because she started calling my home late at night whenever Lester decided to come home for the evening. When she called, and if I answered the telephone, she would hang up. Of course, if the telephone rang again, Lester would run to answer it. Based on the conversation from his end, I knew it was his mistress, even though he said it was one of his colleagues, after hanging up the telephone. She called one day at noon with a disguised voice and asked for Lester. I said he was not at home and asked who was calling. She said he was supposed to meet her for lunch but did not show up. She then had the audacity to say to me, "I am not supposed to talk to you," and hung up the telephone. That stupid and silly statement gave her away, and I knew it was her trying to find Lester.

The day after attending the reception on Capitol Hill, I wrote a "Last Will and Testament," which spelled out who was to take care of Casey upon my death. I also wrote a separate note that said to look into the lives of two people in case I died of a gunshot wound or car accident. I went to the bank, where I had a safety deposit box, and left both the will and note in the box. The next thing I did was to tell Casey that I had a handwritten will and where it could be found in case anything happened to me. Being a very mature young child, she said she would let her Aunt Julie know where the will was located in case anything happened to me. Maybe I was getting too paranoid, but even to this day I believe it was important to take such action in my situation.

I never discussed that particular night with Casey until I started writing this book. By that time, she had grown into a beautiful woman with a great career that took her all over the world. I asked her if she remembered the night I came home and the screen door was locked and her dad ran down the stairs to the door with a gun in his hand. She said yes and had a sad but angry look in her eyes. I told her that I had wondered that evening and many times after if he had planned to shoot me, and if so, why he didn't. She said, "Because he knew I was right behind him and would be a witness if anything happened to you." All these years, I did not know that she also wondered whether he had planned to shoot me. She certainly was mature way beyond her age back in those days.

The day after the reception, I saw Casey off to school and called HUD to see if it had a public housing program. I was lucky that I found a friendly and helpful person in the office of public information who gave me two telephone numbers—one for the general public housing program and one for the Indian Public Housing Program. I called the Indian Public Housing number but was transferred to the Office of the Legal Counsel for the Cabinet Secretary of HUD. I was told this office was in charge of the program.

When the secretary answered the phone, I told her that I was transferred to her from the Indian Housing Office. I went on to tell her that I was calling to see if there were any job openings in the Indian Public Housing Office. I also told her that I had just received my master's degree in architecture and urban planning and had performed a survey on the Navajo Public Housing Program the previous summer. After finishing my story, she put me on hold for a few minutes while she talked to the legal counsel. When she got back on the telephone, she told me there was one job opening for a housing specialist, which was scheduled to close the next day at 5:00 P.M. She went on to say that if I was interested, I needed to get my resume down to her as quickly as possible.

It was only 10:00 A.M. when I found a job opening that fit with my most recent job experience and that was in line with my academic program. I did not want anything to go wrong, so I immediately grabbed a copy of my resume and quickly drove down to the agency. I had to provide my identification and the name of the person I was going to see at the entrance. The guards had to call that office first and confirm my visit with the person I identified. I waited for about ten minutes before the secretary came down to meet me. She was a very helpful and friendly person. She took my resume and said someone would get back to me as soon as a selection was made. I left with a big smile since I knew in my heart they most likely would select me for the job based on my experience and academic degrees.

One week later, I received a call from the Indian Housing Office, informing me that I had been selected for the job. The personnel specialist told me this was an informal selection notice and that the agency's personnel office would be sending me an official letter of my selection within the week. I was so excited and wanted to tell a couple of friends but wanted Casey to be the first to hear, so I waited until she got home. She gave me a big hug and kiss, and we celebrated with a big bowl of ice cream.

Later that evening, I called a couple of friends to let them know of my good news, and they were happy for me. While I was on the telephone, Lester, for some strange reason, evidently had decided to come home and walked into the house around 7:00 P.M. This certainly was not his usual "return home" time if and when he decided to come home. A few minutes later, he came downstairs into the kitchen, where I was fixing popcorn for Casey and me. He must have heard me telling one of my friends of my informal job offer while I was on the telephone. He asked how my job hunting was coming along, and I told him that I received a call that day on my selection for a position with HUD. I told him it was an informal offer and would not be official until I received a letter from agency's personnel office. He neither said, "Congratulations," or "I am happy for you," not that I wanted a pat on the back from him.

The good news on my selection for the job soon vanished into thin air one week later. I received a call from the agency's office of personnel informing me that the Office of Personnel Management (OPM) overturned my selection. One of the responsibilities of this office is to monitor the selection process of all agencies when a federal job is advertised as being open to all candidates from the public and private sector. If the job is open to only candidates within the particular agency that is advertising the job, OPM will not get involved in the selection process. HUD's personnel office informed me that because I was selected over a ten-point veteran, OPM denied my selection. I was surprised and stunned since I was not aware that one could not be selected for a federal position over a ten-point veteran even if he or she were more qualified than the veteran. I asked what I could do, but the personnel specialist said there was nothing the agency or I could do. I hung up the telephone and immediately went to the local library to do some research on federal jobs and the hiring process. The information on qualified veterans was, indeed, correct.

## Chapter 19

I thought about the veterans and the sacrifices they made for our country. I believed very strongly then and today that they deserve to receive benefits from the government. My father and others in my extended family were veterans who fought in various wars. I also knew I could not just sit back and accept the bad situation I was in. I wanted to get back the job that was offered to me and taken away so quickly. I knew in my heart that I would be able to perform the job very well if given the chance; after all, I had the academic credentials and job experience. I started thinking and planning on how to approach the situation and knew that I had to move quickly.

The next morning, after thinking and planning late into the night, I decided to ask for legal help from Charles Burston, special counsel to the Cabinet Secretary of HUD. I was not sure if he could help me, but I decided to take the risk of asking. Later that morning, I called Mr. Burston's office and asked one of his secretaries to speak to him. The secretary wanted to know the reason for the call, so I briefed her about the job I was offered and lost within one week. She said she was familiar with the position since Mr. Burston was also responsible for the Indian Housing Program. She put me on hold for a few seconds and when she returned, she told me that he was in a meeting. She said she would leave a message for him and that he most likely would not return my call until after 5:00 P.M. I did not care what time he returned my call; I was just glad he was willing to talk to me.

It was indeed after 5:00 P.M. when Mr. Burston returned my call. I quickly told him about the informal job offer and that it was denied by OPM because I was selected over a ten-point veteran. He gruffly said, "What do you want me to do?" I quickly and firmly said I wanted his help in getting this job back because I was highly qualified and that he, as a lawyer, should know how to help me. I was young, daring, and took many risks in those days. He softened his tone and wanted me to tell him in detail what happened, which I did for next ten minutes. After our thirty minutes of talk, he said he would look into the matter the next morning and wanted names and telephone numbers of all personnel who had discussed the position with me.

The following week, Mr. Burston called me and said he was currently reviewing the job-hiring process for the agency and for the position that was taken away from me. He further indicated that he would keep me apprised of the findings. I was very pleased to hear from him and to know that he was just not another average federal bureaucrat. Like with any complaint, whether legitimate or not, the federal government started looking into the situation. Not long after that, I was notified by one of my former professors at UCLA that he was called by two agencies to get some information on me. He was not able to give me the specifics but wanted to know if I was in some kind of trouble. I assured him I was not and that it was all related to my complaint about a job that was taken away from me after being selected for it. I was not sure at the time that my background was being checked and whether the veteran's background was also being checked. This would have been the fair and reasonable thing for the investigators to do.

In the third week, Mr. Burston informed me that he had made some progress and that since I was living in the state of Virginia, the outlook for a job looked hopeful. Mr. Burston found a hundred-year-old law, which I call the "Hiring Preference Law," which required a certain number of residents from each state to be given preference in the hiring process.

That same week, Lester asked if I could help out a friend of his who owned a consulting firm in Denver. I told him I needed to stay in the area at the request of Mr. Burston, so there was no further discussion with him on the job. However, the next day Lester's friend, who I knew, called and asked if I could help his company for a couple of weeks in North Dakota. After a lengthy discussion, I agreed to help him, so I called Mr. Burston to let him know I had a job offer for two weeks in North Dakota. He was agreeable to my traveling the next two weeks but wanted me to stay in contact with him during my two-week job stint.

I left on a Sunday morning for Denver to meet with the company and to get briefed on the work I was to perform. I met with the company owner and his staff the next day. After a day of discussions and planning, I left for North Dakota on Tuesday morning. It was good to be away from the miserable life I had in Virginia, but I also missed and was worried about my precious daughter, Casey. I prayed that my husband was taking good care of her and was not leaving her with babysitters every night while he shacked up with his mistress.

The latter part of the second week on the job in North Dakota, the hotel gave me a message to call Mr. Burston as soon as possible. When I called him, he informed me that OPM, the guardian of federal positions, informed him that the State of Virginia had filled their job quota for federal positions for the year. Using the Virginia "job preference law" was now out the door for me. Congress abolished that age-old law the following year during my battle with the federal government. I guess it was useful back in the 1800s, when the federal government was still small. It appears the law was just gathering dust for many years until Mr. Burston used it to get back my job. Mr. Burston, being a tenacious person, said not to be discouraged and wanted me to register to vote in my home state of New Mexico. He said that the state of New Mexico had not reached its quota for federal jobs, and as a resident I would qualify under the state "job preference program." He also suggested I reroute my flight home through Albuquerque so that I could register to vote in my home state.

During that conversation, I finally told Mr. Burston that one or both agencies, OPM and HUD, were investigating my background. I told him a former professor called me to find out if I was in some kind of trouble. I said to Mr. Burston, "I think the investigators are not only doing a background check; they are also checking my academic training and job experiences." I asked Mr. Burston if he could find out if a background check had been completed on the ten-point veteran. This was to find out if the selected employee was indeed a ten-point veteran. Mr. Burston was very surprised about my background check since I had not been officially selected for the position. He said he would check to see if the ten-point veteran had a background check performed. A background check or investigation is required for all individuals who are selected for federal government positions.

It turned out that I did not have to reroute my flight through Albuquerque. The next day, I called the New Mexico Voter Registration Office to find out if I had to register in person or if it had a registration form that could be submitted by mail. I was told I could register by completing and submitting the registration form, so I requested the form to be sent to my home in Virginia. I completed the registration form upon my return to Virginia and sent it back by Federal Express to the office of the New Mexico County Clerk.

## Chapter 20

Before I received a confirmation that I was registered to vote in the state of New Mexico, I received good news. The last week in June 1977, I received a call from Mr. Burston, informing me that I would be getting a call from the HUD personnel office to be followed up with an official letter informing me that I was selected for the housing specialist position. He informed me that he did an inquiry into the ten-point veteran story and found the individual had lied about being a ten-point veteran. He was a veteran, but not a ten-point one. This, of course, bounced him out of the competition, and I was again selected for the position. It was a long, ugly fight with the two agencies, but I had a very intelligent, creative, and tenacious lawyer who believed in me. He was more than willing to help me in the struggle to regain the job that was taken away from me. The official job offer came by letter that same week, and I was requested to report for work on July 5, 1977.

During that same week, Lester came home around 1:00 P.M. and said he was leaving for a trip to California and would not be back until Sunday. I didn't know why he was telling me his schedule since he seldom came home when he returned to the D.C. area from a business trip. While he was preparing his clothes for the trip, I went to the basement to avoid any further face-to-face contact with him. While in the basement, I could hear him talking on the telephone in the kitchen, which was right above where I was sitting. I could hear him requesting in a demanding tone to see the doctor that afternoon. He said it was an emergency, so I got very curious and picked up the telephone in the basement quietly to listen. I got the full scoop on why it was urgent that he see the doctor that afternoon. Upon describing the illness and the very important business trip he was scheduled to take that evening, the doctor's office gave him an afternoon appointment that day.

The first thing that came to my mind was catching some kind of disease from him. I decided I had to leave that house as soon as I got two salary payments, which would not be until the month of August. It was very evident that the man whom I assisted in reaching his goals and who had given me nothing in return had desires to be with the less-than-respectable mistress. I desperately wished I could leave my miserable life that very day but could not do so yet.

On a wonderful morning of July 5, 1977, I reported to the Indian Housing Program as a housing program specialist. The program was brand new, so we only had four staff members, but I understand they have twice that many employees now. It turns out this office reported directly to Mr. Burston. We were located on the seventh floor, and our immediate supervisor, Mr. Burston, was located on the twelfth floor. This meant many daily trips up to the twelfth floor. I often took the stairs up to his office for exercise and to relieve my sadness and stress.

After two weeks on the job, I was requested by Mr. Burston to attend a two-day Indian housing conference in Denver. Although I missed my daughter and was concerned about her care, it was good to attend the conference. A friend who worked for one of the federal agencies in Washington was one of the speakers at the conference, and we were able to have dinner one evening. While having dinner with her, I told her that I was leaving my husband and I found a place to live. She was so shocked to hear my reason for leaving since the story of the affair had not reached her yet. She offered to help Casey and me in any way she could. This friend had also been kind enough to distribute my resume to various organizations during the time I was trying to find a job.

## Chapter 21

I found out that Lester was leaving on a trip the second week in August. So I decided the week he was away would be a good time to move. I quickly notified my move-in date to the management office of the apartment complex where I had reserved space back a couple of months ago. Having worked for one solid month, I could now afford the security deposit and the first month's rent. I looked forward to moving. I discussed our move with Casey one evening and asked her to think once again about putting Snowball in a shelter for adoption rather than having him euthanized. I told her if we took him to a shelter, someone would most likely adopt him, since he was such a loving and beautiful cat. She was adamant about Snowball being euthanized. She said she did not want him adopted because he could end up with mean parents. I was so very sad for her, but I knew she was strong enough to handle it.

Both Casey and I decided that Snowball would be euthanized on Friday the second week of August, since the movers were coming the next day to move a few pieces of furniture and our personal belongings. I made an appointment with the veterinarian to have Snowball euthanized at 6:30 P.M. on Friday evening. I also told Casey to have Snowball put on a leash and have him ready to go to the veterinarian when I got home around 6:00 P.M. That Friday when I arrived home, she had Snowball on a leash and had brushed him really well. I took several pictures of Casey and Snowball as they stood on the front porch just before leaving for the veterinarian's office. We were both very sad but knew it had to be done, and neither one of us said much on the way to the veterinarian's office. I still get sad when I see her in my mind holding Snowball on a leach on the front porch. That image will stay with me the rest of my life.

When we arrived at the veterinarian's office, he and his assistant were waiting for us since we were the last customers of the day. The veterinarian took Casey's hands and said to her, "This will not hurt Snowball, and he will go to sleep really fast." His assistant held her gently as the veterinarian gave Snowball the shot, and he did go to sleep within seconds. The veterinarian and his assistant said they would take care of his body as we had arranged. Casey and I left. I held her all the way to the car, and I wanted to cry so badly, but I knew I had to be strong for Casey. I am sure Casey wanted to cry but felt she had to be strong for her mother. We did not feel like eating dinner when we got home, so we just had some popcorn and Coke.

Later that evening, I went to the basement and cried my heart out for not only Snowball, but for Casey, too. After crying, I cleaned up and helped Casey pack up her toys and other personal things she had accumulated since moving to Virginia. While we were packing, she said she felt sad but knew Snowball had gone to cat heaven. She further stated she did not believe the Catholic nun at her school who said animals did not go to heaven since they had no souls. Casey said there had to be a place in heaven for animals, since Noah was asked by God to pick two types of animals and put them on the ark before the flood came. I was glad she was not so sad, but I am sure her heart was broken just like mine. I had packed the few things we were taking with us during the week, so there was not much to do the last evening in what was supposed to be our home for years to come.

The next day, on a Saturday, we got up early and drove to McDonald's to get some breakfast since all the dishes were packed and ready to be picked up by the movers. We went home and waited for the movers, who came right at 9:00 A.M. as scheduled. I had the movers load a few pieces of furniture since we had rented a small apartment with only one bedroom. The apartment complex was brand new, so everything in the building was clean and beautiful. I made sure that only my chest of drawers in the master bedroom was moved to our new home. I certainly did not want to use anything else from that bedroom, especially the bed he slept in the few times he came home. I did not want us to catch any disease that he contracted while he was gallivanting around with his mistress.

Since we did not have much to move, the two gentlemen moved us to the new apartment within two hours. They made sure everything was set up and in the places we wanted before they left. They probably knew the family was breaking up since they were very kind and probably felt sorry for us. Their kindness was heartwarming since we had no one to turn to in our time of sadness and hardship. But we were also happy to get out of that house and away from the bad karma we had been living under for a little over a year. That period of time seemed like an eternity.

Casey and I spent the reminder of the day unpacking and grocery shopping for the coming week. We were all alone, but surprisingly we were actually happy. My heart was light, and I felt a happiness I had not felt since leaving California. I asked Casey how she was feeling after we got home from the grocery store. She gave me a big smile and said, "I like our apartment, Mom, and I love you very much." She also said she missed Snowball but knew he was in a very safe place where no one would hurt him.

After dinner, we decided to pop Jiffy popcorn, which was very popular in those days. Jiffy popcorn came in a foil container, and you had to move it back and forth slowly over the stove burner to get it to pop. While still living at the other home, we tried many evenings to get it to pop without burning it, but it always burned. We decided to try popping the Jiffy popcorn one more time. It was a miracle that it popped completely without burning. We were so happy that we laughed and danced around in the kitchen.

The weekend was spent preparing for work and for Casey's first day of school. I ran through our schedule with Casey several times that weekend. I was to take her to the school bus stop, which was only two blocks away from home. Once she got on the bus, I was to drive to the public bus stop, where there were parking spaces for commuters to Washington. After school, Casey was to walk home from the bus stop and to telephone me as soon as she got home. I made sure I was in my office every day at the very moment she was scheduled to get home so that I could receive her call.

Because our apartment was in a very safe location, confirmed by some of the parents in the neighborhood I spoke with, I decided it was safe for Casey to walk home after school. Casey became a latchkey child that year, walking home with a boy and a girl from the same school who lived nearby.

## Chapter 22

I threw myself into my work, and the harder I worked, the more tasks I was assigned. I soon found out that Mr. Burston was a perfectionist and he did not accept mistakes or poorly prepared assignments well. If you were not swift on your feet, he did not channel much work your way and had very little communication with you. Having lived in a very strict household as a child and with a father who was very demanding, I learned long ago to move and respond quickly to any tasks and questions thrown my way. As children, my father reminded us continuously that in order to be successful in the "white man's world," we had to be twice as good as the "white man." I reminded myself of my father's philosophy for many years after leaving home and set my standards very high. However, I also knew that certain things could not be accomplished within the very high standards I established for myself. I found out that my father's philosophy was true to some extent and may still be true today for many minorities in this country, even though we, as a country, have come a long way.

Keeping my father's philosophy in mind, I worked hard and quickly for Mr. Burston. However, like any new employee, I made some mistakes. One late afternoon, just before the end of the workday, I received a call from Mr. Burston's secretary to come to his office. I asked what the meeting was about, but she did not know. Immediately I sensed this was not going to be a good meeting, so I grabbed a copy of my latest assignment, which was referred to as the "white paper," and rushed to his office. He did not respond to my "Good afternoon" but waved me to a chair instead.

Mr. Burston said my analysis of the Indian Housing Program was not up to par. He stated briskly that the basis for my conclusion was not supported very well. He wanted facts and statistics on why government public housing was not adequate for Indians living on federal reservations. I noted my position and started citing facts and statistics that were identified in my analysis. I had also included information on the cultural traditions of Native Americans.

During this heated discussion, I stated in a brisk tone that the Native-American culture was never included in any of the decisions made by white society, especially made by the federal government. He was more than upset with my statement, and he spent the next half-hour citing treaties, legal decisions, rules, and regulations that were related to Native Americans across North America. I did not win the argument, nor did I make any brownie points that afternoon. He requested that I redraft and resubmit the "white paper" the next day by noon. As I was leaving, I said to myself ever so softly, "If I survive under this attorney, I can succeed in any job anywhere in the world."

During my tenure with Mr. Burston, I received in the mail a letter from a company in Texas, seeking people with architecture and urban planning degrees to work in Saudi Arabia. The description of the job looked exciting, and the starting salary was far better than what I was earning with the federal government. Since I had a master's degree in architecture and urban planning, I was more than ready to work in that country. After telling the company that I was interested, they sent me brochures on living and working in Saudi Arabia. I was to live in a compound with other Americans and would have to wear a headscarf and clothing that covered my entire body at all times. My daughter could not live with me but would be sent to a private school in Switzerland or England. The brochure said the company would pay for the private school for her. After finding out that she could not live with me, I dropped all dreams of working in Saudi Arabia. My daughter says she would have loved going to a private school in Switzerland and that I may have missed a great opportunity. I think I made the right decision not to go to Saudi Arabia.

One week after Casey and I moved into our new home, Marcey, my friend who worked in the same agency as Lester, called me. She wanted to let me know that it was Lester's last week with the agency. She said he was leaving to serve as the executive director of a Native-American organization in Denver. This horrible man who I supported through his graduate years and followed him all over the country never called me. Although he did not have our new unlisted telephone number, he knew my office number. He could have called my office to find out how Casey, his only child, was doing and where he could call her or send her letters, but he never even bothered to find her. She never asked about him, either, so I think she was glad she did not have to see or talk to him.

A few days after he left the area, Marcey called to let me know that one of her staff members informed her that his mistress was leaving her job. According to her staff member, Lester's mistress said she was going west to take it easy for a while. I don't know if Lester asked her to join him in Denver or if she insisted on joining him at his new location.

Several weeks after Lester left the area, I asked Marcey to get his new office number for me so that he could stay in touch with Casey. I thought it was only right that I give our home number to Lester so he could call Casey every week. I had promised myself that I would always keep the communication channel open between him and Casey, no matter how I felt. As I promised myself, I kept this communication channel open for the next six years, but he never called Casey, nor did he send her any letters or cards. He never called or visited her while he was on business trips to Washington. He never sent any gifts to her on her birthday or at Christmas time. In fact, he never even provided any financial support until almost two years after he moved to Colorado. If you can call this support, it was only a hundred dollars a month, which came sporadically. I guess, in the meantime, his mistress, who never lifted a hand to help him in any way, was being pampered and living high on the hog.

Many deadbeat fathers are not able to get away with not paying child support today because there are laws that permit law enforcement organizations to hunt them down and get them to pay or go to jail. Some states have passed laws that allow the garnishment of salaries. Salary may be garnished when a person falls behind on their federal or state taxes, on their child support payments, court fees, and even student loans. Lester got away "scot free" since there were no such laws during that period of time. I also contributed to Lester's deadbeat behavior because I did not demand child support, which I did only because I wanted him to keep in touch with Casey. I knew if I demanded support payments, he would definitely not make any attempt to see or communicate with Casey. Despite my efforts not to demand child support, he still did not make any attempts to stay in touch with his daughter. After six years of trying to keep the communication channels open for him, I realized he did not care for her welfare. So I closed that chapter forever after Casey made it clear she had no desire to see or talk to him. That was one of the best decisions that both Casey and I made during her formative years.

The first Christmas in our apartment was a happy time for us, even though we were still on a very tight budget. I had saved some funds through my Christmas savings account at my bank, so I was able to buy several small gifts for Casey. She wanted to buy me a Christmas gift, so I gave her some money, and we went shopping one evening. She bought me my favorite perfume, Shalimar by Guerlain. On Christmas Day, we baked a couple of Cornish hens with cornbread stuffing. It was a wonderful day. I was very sad for her because her dad did not even bother to call or send her a Christmas present. She was, nonetheless, very happy. Two close friends called us and wished us a Merry Christmas and Happy New Year. We never heard from my family, and I assumed they were upset about my separation. However, I thought they would at least call us during the holidays since they knew we were now alone. I made excuses for them in my mind and dismissed their silence.

In March of 1978, I had to go to Denver for a two-day conference, so I thought it would be great to take Casey with me so she could see her dad. We had not heard from him since he left the end of August in 1977 and did not know where he lived. However, I did know where his office was located. I wanted Casey's visit to be a surprise, so we flew to Denver without telling her dad that she was coming.

Casey really enjoyed our flight from Washington National Airport, now known as Ronald Reagan Washington National Airport, to the Denver International Airport. Our flight arrived in the early afternoon as scheduled. After we settled in our hotel, I called Lester at the office to let him know that I brought Casey with me for a two-day conference in Denver. He did not sound too pleased and wanted to know why I brought her. I got angry and said very harshly, "Don't you want to see your daughter, whom you have not seen in a long time?" I went on to tell him that he was the sorriest excuse of a father since he never telephoned her, never sent her any gifts, cards, or letters, did not see her while he was on business trips to Washington, and did not even support her financially. I ended the conversation by telling him that I would be visiting an attorney on that issue upon our return to Washington.

He finally agreed to take her to lunch the next day. After providing the address of where Casey could be located, a time was arranged and he duly collected her the following day. When Casey returned, I asked her how the lunch went, to which she replied it went okay. Never did he bother to show Casey where he lived or any insight into his life. Instead he dropped off the daughter he had not seen for close to a year, and that was that. Later, we learned he was sharing a home with his mistress, and they were both expecting a baby. His priorities, I guess, were elsewhere now.

In the summer of 1978, while going over some completed task assignments, Mr. Burston asked me if I had ever thought of going to law school. I told him I was not interested and that the costs outweighed the benefits. He said, "You have a great legal mind and will do very well in law school." I was shocked to hear that coming from him but was very flattered by such a compliment from a very wise and intelligent man. He further indicated that I did not have to practice law but could use what I learned in law school in any kind of job I held. He said going to night school could be the answer to holding costs down and for me to think about it very seriously.

I did think seriously about going to law school, and a year later, I stared my legal studies to use in my job and not as a practicing attorney. I entered the night program so that I could continue working. Mr. Burston's advice was among the best I had ever received, and he was right about using it in my job. Several years later, I completed my legal studies and have been using what I learned in every job I have held in my career. Working for Mr. Burston was, indeed, one of the greatest challenges, but I found him to be a kind man under the tough exterior.

Two weeks after Mr. Burston discussed going to law school with me, our office was notified that the Indian Housing Program was being transferred to the regular public housing program. Mr. Burston called the staff into a meeting one July morning and informed us of the news. Our program was to remain as a separate office within that division. He said we would be reporting to Mr. Sherrett for the day-to-day operations of the program. Mr. Burston also informed us that the agency hired a Native-American man as special assistant to the Cabinet Secretary of HUD for the Indian Housing Program. He thanked us for our services and introduced Mr. Sherrett who briefed us on the new office policies and our new office home. We were informed that HUD's Office of the Special Assistant was a policy office and the special assistant would be reporting directly to the agency's cabinet secretary and would not be involved with the day-to-day housing operations.

## Chapter 23

In the fall of 1978, I received my divorce papers by registered mail. The papers stated the reason for the divorce was that I continually quarreled with the plaintiff (Lester), causing him to suffer extreme mental anguish. I laughed and cursed when I read the phrase "mental anguish" because that was what I said I would use if I divorced him back when we were going to school in California. I also got very angry because the divorce complaint was not true. I had not seen or talked to this horrible man for over a year. In addition, I hardly saw the man during my last year of graduate school in California and the miserable year in Virginia when he rarely came home. This made three years when I was virtually absent from his life, so it was impossible for me to have "continually quarreled with him," as the divorce papers stated.

I tore up the divorce papers and threw them in the trash bin on the way to work. The papers did state that I would have full custody of Casey and that Lester was willing to pay one hundred dollars a month. Wow, he was finally willing to give me a measly hundred dollars a month which, of course, I knew would not be paid in a timely manner. The papers also stated that he would be awarded reasonable visitation rights. This was laughable, too, since he never visited or communicated with his only daughter on his own initiative.

I knew a second set of divorce papers would be forthcoming again, but I was not quite sure whether to sign them or not. I thought of getting an attorney and fighting back. The decision to get an attorney and get a divorce on the grounds of adultery would have been fair and reasonable. But it would have been ugly, costly, and not good for Casey. And at this point in time, I still was hopeful that Casey and her father would develop a good father-daughter relationship again. I decided seeking a divorce based on his adultery would destroy any hope for that good relationship.

The divorce complaint caused me to temporarily get malicious. I thought of filing an Alienation of Affection lawsuit against the mistress for interfering in my marriage. However, Virginia did not allow for that.

The second set of divorce papers arrived on December 18, 1978, one week before Christmas. When I picked up the certified letter with a return receipt on a Monday morning, I knew what they were. By now I had decided to sign even though the reason for the divorce was a lie. I just wanted him out of my life. I quickly read them, confirming they were the same as the last copy, so I signed the papers there at the post office and sent them right back.

I drove to work that day since the public bus I normally take had already left the "kiss and ride" area, and I did not want to be late. On the way to work, I wondered why I had stayed so long with this man who lied and cheated so much. I guess he wanted to come out looking honorable and decent, which he was not. It was Christmas, and everyone seemed to be cheerful, and I was determined to give my precious daughter a wonderful time during her Christmas and New Year school break.

Casey and I, indeed, did have a good Christmas, even though we were alone. And as usual, not one family member called us, and we did not call anyone except for a couple of friends in the area. Lester, now my ex-husband, did not send Christmas gifts to Casey, as usual, but by now, she did not want to see or hear from her dad.

Casey and I got up early to prepare our feast for the day. We got all the cooking utensils that we needed for our cooking fiesta. The next five hours were spent baking and cooking. We had so much fun fixing our turkey dinner on Christmas Day. It felt good to enjoy a meal together and dare to look forward a little to the year ahead, while I reflected quietly on how much my daughter had experienced at such a young age. How she was dealing with a father who did not even think enough of his child to send presents.

After dinner, we went to a movie. It felt good to get out of the house, but for some reason, it was a scary movie. When we returned home later that evening, Casey had me check behind doors, her closet, and under her bed.

Monsters aside, we had a great Christmas and one I hoped would shepherd us toward better times ahead. It was, indeed, a great day, and we knew for sure that everything was going to work out fine for us.

## Chapter 24

I had the wonderful feeling that 1979 was going to be far better than 1978 for both of us. Things were going really well at work and home. Casey was doing very well in school and had adjusted to our new home and neighborhood. My job under the new supervisor was going very well but not too well with the special assistant for the Indian Housing Program. Although he did not have the day-to-day responsibilities for the housing program, many Native-American organizations and housing authorities went directly to him for solutions and answers. Since he did not know the rules, regulations, and policies, he would call us for answers. I found out very quickly that he did not like my answers or solutions, even though they were in line with federal housing rules and regulations. As the only woman on staff, I did not have any kind of support from my male colleagues. I was often ostracized or ridiculed behind my back.

One scary incident still rings in my mind today. When our program was under Mr. Burston, one older man on our staff by the name of Harry was not very well liked or given much work by Mr. Burston. Every week, Harry found it necessary to tell the rest of the staff and a contractor who shared our office space that I was Mr. Burston's favorite employee because I was a woman. I ignored his silly innuendos, and I did not make the time to sit down and have a discussion with him because I was swamped with work every day of the week. One evening, I stayed late to complete a very important assignment. The contractor who shared office space with us also stayed late. I had been told that he retired from the Central Intelligence Agency and was working as a consultant to one of the directors down the hall, although I never saw him do any kind of work or go to any meetings.

I was deep into my work that evening when all of a sudden; the contractor was standing by my cubicle, shouting at me. I was so startled, I jumped and looked up at him, and his eyes were big and red. He said, "Who do you think you are, anyway? You get all the attention and work, and you have embarrassed my friend

Harry." He ranted and raved for what appeared to be an eternity. I was not only dumbfounded, but also frightened. I knew it would not be wise to say anything. I was also afraid to get up and leave for fear he would hit me, so I just sat there until he finished. After he finished, he stormed out of the room.

I sat there for a few minutes to calm myself and allow my knees to stop shaking, and I asked myself, "If I am Mr. Burston's favorite employee, how come he loads me down with work?"

Determined to complete my work, I finished the task at hand and then walked down the dark halls. I hoped to see the director in his office, and fortunately for me, he was there. Not as fortunate for the contractor as I informed the director of what had just taken place. I was told not to worry, as the man would be moving in the next couple of weeks. I could easily have filed a complaint against him, but I chose to see if he was going to move. Looking back, there are times when I have wished I had filed a complaint against him. As a contractor, he would have been fired.

Indeed, the contractor was moved out of our office, and I never reported the incident to Mr. Burston. No longer listening to the contractor making sexist comments about women anymore, I could work a little easier.

During this period of time, women were making their way into high management positions, and our agency had a few in top-level positions. This was obviously devastating to the contractor and his friend Harry, so they would sit there and degrade the female managers almost every day. I was so happy to see the contractor being moved out one wonderful morning, and I never saw the man again anywhere in the building.

One time, the executive director of a Native-American organization from Denver called the special assistant for the Indian Housing Program and complained about me. Evidently, the special assistant was informed that I was not willing to bend the rules for a particular Native-American tribe and he wanted me to be removed from my position. The special assistant called me into his office and immediately went into a tirade. He ended his yelling by telling me that he had the authority to have me removed from my position. Being yelled at like this was the proverbial straw breaking the camel's back. I was no longer willing to cater to his insecurities and egotistical attitude. He often called me into his office on minor issues and to remind me that he held a powerful position and that his authority was equivalent to a Chief Executive Officer in the private sector. He had become a drain. Shoving my chair back, I drew myself to full height, inhaling as I did so. I had enough. "You just do that, and you will have the biggest fight on your hands!" My voice spat at him. Neither he nor I had the authority to bend the housing policies and regulations. I told him that I could file a complaint against him for bending the rules and have him removed from office. As I walked out, I said to him, "You might want to get the facts before you speak to your supervisor and my supervisor before requesting my removal."

## The Forgotten American

Later that week, I was told he was caught trying to bend certain housing policies and was disciplined by Mr. Burston, who was still serving as special counsel to the cabinet secretary of HUD. I was prepared to fight for what was right; however, providence won over, and I did not have to.

The latter part of the summer months, I was requested to attend a housing conference in Oklahoma City. While at the conference, I met a wonderful man by the name of Melvin, who was a member of the board of directors for a housing program. He worked in the private sector but remained attached to the Native-American world through committees and various boards involved in Native-American affairs. Being six feet three inches tall and a former semi-pro football player, he appeared to have no insecurities and certainly was not egotistical. It was easy to communicate with him, and we immediately became friends.

By mid-summer, I had gotten tired of dealing with the special assistant to the Indian Housing Authorities and the Native-American organizations lobbying on behalf of the housing authorities. Toward the end of the summer of my second year on the job I decided it was, indeed, time to leave. The job I enjoyed so much was now becoming a drag and also an unhealthy environment for me. My objectivity was slowly eroding, and I knew I could no longer be effective in working with the Native-American people. They needed someone else to take my place to help them understand and improve the Indian housing bureaucracy.

That fall, I decided I had a better chance of reaching my goals in the non-Native-American workforce. Because I wanted to make a contribution to society as a public servant, I narrowed my search for a job in other federal agencies. I wanted to help the public without being seen as an enemy or as a rival. I wanted to be able to compete for all jobs I sought and not to be given one because I happened to be a minority. I wanted to use my academic credentials to the fullest. I wanted to realize my goals as quickly as I could. After all, so much money and time had gone into attaining my degrees.

So in September of 1979, I left the Native-American work environment forever. I felt guilty and also sad to leave it behind, but I knew that was the best solution for me and the Native-American people. I also knew I would be facing discrimination and possibly hostile people in the environment I chose to be a part of for the rest of my career. Having grown up in the Southwest during the height of racial discrimination, I knew I could face the challenges. Racial discrimination still existed at that time in many federal agencies, but it was not as open and harsh as it was back when I was growing up. I was determined to succeed in the "white man's world" and to give my daughter, Casey, a comfortable, stable, and happy environment.

## Chapter 25

After applying to a couple of agencies, I accepted a job with the U. S. Commission on Civil Rights, which was totally different from the Indian Housing Program. The employees were very polite and cheerful. We all had private offices with doors that could be closed when necessary. However, the work was still in the area of public service.

The Civil Rights Commission is responsible for investigating issues concerning the civil rights of American citizens. It is an independent, executive, bipartisan, fact-finding agency. Its mission is to inform both the U.S. President and Congress on the implementation of civil rights' protections.

I joined the Office of Policy Review, which performed field surveys, collected data from the field, researched voting practices of state governments, and prepared reports on the findings to the U.S. President and Congress. I very much enjoyed my new job and the pleasant atmosphere of the agency. The camaraderie was great, and everyone seemed to work as a team. The agency also seemed to be racially balanced, and everyone had advanced degrees in various fields.

One day in late November, a friend who owned his own company in Washington called me and wanted to know if I knew anyone willing to come to Washington to work for his organization. He wanted a Native-American man or woman who did not mind traveling all over the United States to assist small businesses operated by Native Americans. I said I would look around and get back to him within a week.

I called Melvin and informed him of the job. Melvin and I had remained in touch after meeting each other at the conference in Oklahoma City. He was very much interested in the job and said he had no problem with traveling. Melvin also wanted to know if I had made a decision regarding his marriage proposal, which was made prior to November. I had made a decision the week before to marry him but had not yet told him. I decided this was the right time to tell him. I decided to marry him because he was a very calm, patient, and loving man, and treated Casey like his own daughter. So on that day, while discussing his interest in the job, I told him I would marry him but wanted to continue dating for a while. He applied for the job, was selected for it, and arrived in Washington shortly thereafter. We were married several months later. Since we both had been married before, we did not want a grand ceremony. We had a small private wedding with only a few friends in attendance. Casey was very happy for us and happy to have a father figure in our home again.

One day in mid-September, 1980, I received a call from Alvin, a friend and lawyer who was the director of Indian Affairs at the U.S. Department of Energy. Alvin was attending the UCLA School of Law when I was an undergraduate student at Cal State in the early 1970s. He wanted to know if I would be interested in joining his staff to help Native-American tribes and organizations with contracts and grants awarded to them by the Department of Energy. Although I had previously made a decision to stay away from work related to Native Americans, I told him I would consider it. He wanted me to make a decision within one week.

Alvin also warned me in advance that due to the downsizing of the federal government that year, my position could be abolished or the entire office could be abolished. He also said he needed my help and to give it some serious thought. It was indeed a hard decision since I loved my job at the Civil Rights Commission. After giving the offer some serious consideration, I decided to join his staff because I felt a need to help not only my friend but also the Native-American people once again.

## Chapter 26

So in the last week of September 1980, I resigned from my position at the Civil Rights Commission and joined Alvin's staff in October. I look back to those days with pride because I was able to juggle many tasks at the same time. I had not only taken on a new job, I was a newlywed, attending law school at night and taking care of both Melvin and Casey. I loved the daily multitasking because it gave me the energy and stamina to work toward accomplishing my goals.

My home life was peaceful and full of happiness. Casey was happy to have a father once again, and I was happy to have a loving husband who believed in the family doing things together. Weekends were full of family activities such as tennis games, going to movies, going out to dinner, and other family-oriented activities. My husband and I went to many receptions on Capitol Hill and other places in Washington, D.C., where we met many wonderful people.

As Alvin had warned me, within less than a year on the job, every program within the agency was notified that the budget was cut severely. Everyone was given a written notice, informing us that some programs and positions could be abolished. In the latter part of the summer, we were all notified that there was not enough money to keep all programs running. As a result, the Department of Energy had to begin the reduction-in-force process immediately. Our director, Alvin, was a political appointee, and we were sure he would be one of many to be asked to leave his position. The latter part of August, he resigned from his position before the agency requested him to leave. He accepted an offer to join a small law firm not far from our location. He assured us that top management promised not to abolish the Indian Affairs Program Office. But we knew certain positions within our office would most likely be targeted for termination.

Many federal employees were beginning to panic, and we found out through the media that a few had committed suicide because they either were going to lose their jobs or had lost their jobs. One day in September, a colleague told us that a man went up to the roof of the HUD building and jumped to his death because he had been informed his services was no longer required. Because I was the newest of the four staff members within the Office of Indian Affairs, I knew deep in my heart that I would be receiving a pink slip. Sure enough, I received the notice two weeks in advance of my position being abolished. It said my position was ended due to the agency's budget cuts. I appealed the agency's termination decision to the Merit Systems Protection Board (MSPB). The MSPB is an independent, bipartisan guardian of the merit systems under which federal employees work. The agency's decision to abolish my position was upheld, as I already knew it would be.

The summer before I was forced to leave my position, I had completed law school. Nevertheless, there was still the internship to complete. In spite of federal agency cutbacks in many areas of the government, I managed to intern at the Legal Advocate Center in D.C. Completed after Christmas, I was ready to resume job hunting early 1981. With no plans on board to become an attorney, I nevertheless wanted to work in a field that allowed me to utilize my knowledge. A career change was therefore needed, which meant toppling back down the pay structure again. I would be starting over, but I knew in my heart the risk was worth taking. In a few years, I would be making what I earned at my termination. I was young and ambitious. It was no big deal.

Every federal agency now had a slim budget, so it was hard to find a job. I searched high and low in the Metropolitan Washington area for several months without any success. One day I realized it would be easier to get a job at the Department of Energy, where I was terminated. I determined the agency would be more than willing to rehire me for a job since my termination was solely on the basis of the agency's budget cut.

Shortly before finding a job, I became very frightened that I would not be able to find one within the timeframe I was allowed to receive unemployment checks. I became depressed and could not sleep well at night for about a week. I also became very fearful, and at times my body would go limp as if I had no energy. One morning after my husband left for work and Casey had gone to school, I sat down and cried for one solid hour. I asked God why so many negative things were happening in my life. After crying, I cleaned up and scolded myself for being so weak. I told myself that I was a strong person and I had been through very tough times before. I reminded myself that I had a beautiful, healthy daughter and a wonderful husband and therefore should not feel sorry for myself. I went to work on refining my resume and searching various newspapers for job vacancies the rest of the day.

## Chapter 27

One day I saw an advertisement in *The Washington Post* for an entry-level position in the field of federal acquisitions at the Department of Energy. I applied for the position and was selected at the low government salary level I started at when I first began my career. This was fine with me since I did not have much job experience in the field of federal acquisitions. However, I did have a lot of knowledge from an academic standpoint since I had just completed law school. Thus, I knew I could handle the entry-level job. I was back in the federal workforce seven months after being terminated. I wanted to be successful in this field, so I started studying the subject matter immediately.

My job was very interesting, and I was just so happy to be working again. My personal life was great. My married life was wonderful, and my daughter was very happy to have a father figure in the house. In previous years, I had tried my best to get her to go see her dad in Colorado, but she simply refused. She said she did not like being around his mistress, now his wife, or any of his family members, including extended relatives. I stopped pressuring her after I remarried, and we lived as one happy family thereafter. The three of us would play tennis every evening on weekends, and Casey loved playing the game with her new father figure. She loved him very much and treated him as though he was her birth father. He also loved her very much and said many times he was happy to have gained a daughter.

That fall, while Melvin was traveling on the West Coast, Casey and I went house hunting on a weekend. Although Melvin and I talked about purchasing a new home, we never seemed to have the time to search for one. Casey and I found a three-story townhouse that would give the three of us a lot of space. The new home was about ten miles from our apartment and within a short walking distance to Casey's school bus stop. She was still attending a private Catholic school but one that was quite a distance from our home and, thus, entailed a long commute every day.

The price of the home was reasonable, and this was probably because it was next to a large apartment complex with many unsupervised children and teenagers. I have found through the years that many realtors are never completely truthful when asked about a community when purchasing a home. In our case, the realtor said there were a few children in the apartment complex next door, which we found was not true. There were many unsupervised children and teenagers. As first-generation latchkey children, they caused problems. They would come into our neighborhood and skate in the parking lot or knock down trash bins on trash pickup day.

Melvin liked the new home, and after some discussion; we decided to purchase it even though the loan interest rates were very high at the time. We needed more space in our home, and I had enough savings for the down payment. In those days, the required down payments for new homes were still low. I remember withdrawing twenty-five thousand dollars from my savings account to make the down payment. When I look back today, I see that I was beginning to do the same thing that I did in my first marriage. Instead of asking my husband to help with the down payment for the new home, I volunteered to come up with the money.

As I did in my first marriage, I was thinking of Melvin's wellbeing instead of my own. One would think I had learned my lesson from my first marriage, but evidently I had not. I was thinking of the child support he had to pay for his two sons, and that was why I volunteered to pay the down payment, which was not the right thing to do. Yes, as mothers, we need to take care of our children and husbands, but we must also put ourselves at the forefront and take care of ourselves as well.

The three of us were very happy in our new home and did many things together. The one thorn in my side was the fact that Casey's biological father was not communicating with her or providing the monthly support he had agreed to provide. Of course, the child support was never on time, and after a period of time he got so far behind that he owed over two thousand dollars.

## Chapter 28

One evening I mentioned to Melvin how unhappy I was that Casey's father did not try to communicate with her or provide the monthly child support. I told him that he now owed a significant amount. Before I finished my story, Melvin said he wanted to adopt her because he was more of father to her than her biological father. We discussed this further and decided to let Casey, who was then a teenager, know of the adoption. We wanted her to decide if that is what she wanted. She immediately said yes, that she definitely wanted to be adopted, which we knew was best for her.

I made sure I got the child support money before I gave my ex-husband the news of Casey's adoption. The money I knew would not be easy to get without getting my attorney involved, but I gave it a try one day. By this time, my ex-husband, his wife, and their two children were back in Washington, D.C. Evidently, the organization he was running went bankrupt, and he returned to work for the federal agency that employed him when he first came to Washington.

I called him one evening to ask for the full amount of child support Casey was due. I told him I had discussed this with my attorney even though I had not contacted her yet. I told him she would be getting in touch with him the next day. He immediately said he did not have any savings but could get the funds from his credit card the next day. He did get the funds and sent them by Federal Express to Casey within twenty-four hours. So I did not have to put my attorney on notice.

Several weeks after that, I once again called Lester and informed him that my husband wanted to adopt Casey and that she was agreeable to this. By now, the adoption papers were being prepared by our attorney, so I let him know that he would be receiving the papers within the next two weeks. I told him this was best for Casey because he did not provide adequate child support, nor did he ever attempt to communicate with her by telephone or letter and did not even visit her while he was in Washington on business. I also said it was unconscionable that he did not even bother to telephone or visit Casey after returning to work in the Washington, D.C., area.

Lester, whom I considered to be a deadbeat dad, did not put up much of a fight against the adoption. I guess he knew he did not have a chance of winning, or maybe he could no longer afford to provide the support. In any event, the adoption went through smoothly. Once he signed the paper, he was now completely out of our lives, and it was a good feeling. I don't know why I tried so hard and for so long to keep the communication channels open, even though Lester never bothered to use them. I just kept hoping that he would one day call her or visit her, but it never happened. I don't regret it, though, because I know I did my best in trying to get him and Casey to have that father-daughter relationship that once existed, and I can now live with myself.

Casey never wanted to visit him again after her first visit to his home in Colorado. She did not want to write or call him, either, and I was very sad about it. I also did not understand how he could just toss aside his own flesh and blood and provide a comfortable life for the woman who had a reputation as loose and easy. I would have fought tooth and nails for my dear Casey. I kept hoping he would change his ways, but he never did.

Would I try to keep communications open between my daughter and her dad today? I probably would try for a while but not for as long as I did during those years. It is always best to think of your children first when your family is shattered and it becomes necessary to terminate the marriage. If things don't work out in the end, you know you gave it your best for the sake of your children instead of seeking revenge for yourself. One must remember that what goes around comes around. The Supreme Being, whether we call him God, the Holy Spirit, or by other names, will always watch over you.

## Chapter 29

In the spring of 1981, while working at the Department of Energy, I met Nadia, a woman who worked near my office but not in the same department. Nadia asked me one day to go to lunch with her, where we briefed each other on our careers. She said she had a friend who was director of administration at the National Aeronautical and Space Administration (NASA) who was looking for qualified women to work there. This woman worked at one of NASA's field offices located in Greenbelt, Maryland, just outside of the Washington, D.C., beltway. Back in the early 1980s, men still heavily dominated the workforce at the Goddard Space Flight Center, and the director of administration was seeking to fill more positions with women. Evidently, the director wanted more employees with legal and financial backgrounds to work in NASA's Federal Acquisition Department. Nadia believed that with my legal education, I would be more than qualified to work in that department. She asked if I would be interested in applying for a position that was currently vacant. I told her I was very much interested. Nadia said she would let her friend know of my interest and offered to get me a copy of a vacancy announcement.

Upon receiving a copy of the announcement, I updated my resume and submitted it to NASA. A couple of weeks later, I was requested to meet with the chief of the Federal Acquisition Department for an interview. Goddard Space Flight Center was sixty miles from my home. Everything went so fast that I had not had a chance to discuss this with Melvin or Casey.

I went to the interview, which I felt went very well. I was asked to give a brief summary of my career goals and myself. Questions posed by the panel of three men were not difficult to answer. And the panel was not intimidating. A week later, NASA's personnel office called to let me know that I was selected for the job and that Federal Express would send a written notification. I was more than elated to be selected from among a number of applicants. I was also extremely proud since I was the first Navajo Indian woman to work for NASA, an outstanding and respected agency.

I discussed the job offer with Melvin and Casey, and they both thought it was great and that I should accept the offer. However, I was hesitant since I would be driving long distances and was concerned about leaving very early in the morning and coming home late in the evening. As always, I was concerned about Casey. Melvin said not to worry about Casey since she was a very levelheaded girl and the long commute may not be bad as described by many in the area. After a good discussion with my family and a good night's sleep, I accepted the job offer from NASA.

Getting a new job is very exciting but also scary. I reported to NASA on a Monday morning. The traffic on the way to the Goddard Space Flight Center seemed to flow pretty fast; it was not bad at all. After reporting to the personnel office, I was taken to my new job location. Immediately I knew why the director of administration was trying to recruit women. It was, indeed, male dominated, and all the men appeared to be over six feet tall.

I was introduced to the contracting people, engineers, and scientists, who were all affiliated with the NASA space shuttle program. There was one lone woman, and was I ever so happy to meet her. She was the financial wizard for the program and one of the best I have ever known. All personnel affiliated with this particular space shuttle program were located in a two-story building.

Everyone working for this program had to have a top-secret clearance, and since I only had a secret clearance, I was asked to work on federal contracts that did not require a top-secret clearance. The NASA Security Office had agreed to have me come on board with only a secret clearance while my top-secret clearance was being processed. During the first week on the job, I completed all the required paperwork for a top-secret clearance, as well as the necessary medical exams and fingerprints.

Two weeks later, I was asked by my supervisor to go to the security office for another fingerprinting session. I was scared and began to wonder if this had to do with all the protest marches I participated in during my college years. On the walk over to the security office, I asked my supervisor why I had to have another fingerprinting session. He said he did not know, but it could be because some of my fingerprints did not come out clearly. I was even more frightened, so I asked him, "What if this second set does not take? Will they fire me?" He laughed really loudly and said, "Don't worry; it will be done correctly this time, and you will not be fired." This man was one of the best supervisors I ever had. Indeed, the second set of fingerprints came out clearly, and I eventually received my clearance.

My colleagues at NASA were all male, and they did not offer any help with anything. Of course, I was used to that by now, so it really did not bother me. I enjoyed working there, but I also faced many challenges. Six months after arriving, I negotiated and awarded a very large contract with a large engineering company. The day of negotiations, I walked into the conference room with my pricing analyst (the financial wizard) and was shocked to find twenty white men in their pinstripe suits. I also heard some snickering in the corner while I was walking to the head of the table. I am sure the snickering men did not expect a short minority woman to lead a negotiation session. They probably found it rather funny. This was not amusing to me, but I chose to ignore it and got the negotiation session started.

A week before the negotiation session, I had requested that the company president bring only people who could contribute to the negotiation session. I also asked that one person be designated as the company lead negotiator and that he have the authority to commit the company to a contract price. I had requested the company not to bring its attorney to the session and that if and when it became necessary to get our attorneys involved, I would set up a separate session.

We negotiated all morning and late into the afternoon. During this session, there were several young men sitting in the corner who chatted and laughed during our session. By the end of the day, I was very annoyed at the disrespectful behavior of these individuals, and I asked the president and his assistants to stay behind for a few minutes. Once everyone had departed, I gave him a list of six people who could return to the second negotiation session the next day. I also told him the young men in the corner were very rude, made no contribution to the day's session, and would not be allowed to return. He did not agree with my request and wanted everyone back. He said he wanted them to learn from this session for future projects. I informed him that this was not a training session, and I would cancel the negotiation session if they returned the next day. We ended up agreeing on who should return from his company.

I really did not understand why the president of the company wanted an entourage when NASA had only two people, me as the authorized representative of the federal government and my pricing analyst, who was much sharper than their three financial wizards. Although he agreed to comply with my request, he evidently complained to my supervisor that same evening. The next morning, my supervisor wanted to know why I dismissed some company personnel from my session. I gave him the full scoop. All he said was, "I figured so, and I told the president that you had full authority to make the necessary decisions." The president did not go any further with his complaint.

During my tenure with NASA, both my mother and oldest sister died within six months of each other. My mother had breast cancer and suffered for several years. Since her cancer had metastasized, we knew she would leave us one day. However, the death of my oldest sister was a shock to me. She was not ill but had been admitted to the hospital to have a non-cancerous tumor removed from the base of her neck. She had promised me that she was going to be fine and she was having minor surgery. She died within a couple of days after the surgery from a collapsed lung and not due to the surgery. I was so sad about my mother and sister dying that I cried every day on the way to work for many months. In addition, my second marriage, which I truly believed would, indeed, be for life, was beginning to fall apart. Melvin, who traveled a great deal, was beginning to fly home on Saturday or Sunday evenings instead of on Friday evenings as he did before.

## Chapter 30

One early morning, while standing in line at the voting place, Melvin quickly said, "By the way, did I tell you I will be home on Sunday evening?" I immediately got angry but could not say much since we were in a public place. I had agreed to drive him to the airport that morning in his car. I never liked driving his car because he always purchased large vehicles. We voted, and I drove him to the airport but said very little to him, and he knew I was angry. On Sunday evening, I picked him up and again, I said very little to him. He wanted to have dinner at one of our favorite restaurants, so we had dinner at the place that was closest to home.

While having dinner, he wanted to know why I was angry. I told him that he had no excuse for coming home on Saturdays or Sundays and I wanted him to start coming home on Friday evenings like normal people who traveled. I should have asked why he stayed through Saturday in Albuquerque, but I did not. I have no idea to this day why I did not ask a lot of questions that most wives would ask. This one particular trip began the erosion of our marriage. He never said he would start coming home from his trips on Friday evenings. I promised myself that if he did it one more time, I would ask him to leave our home.

I guess Melvin thought I forgot my request for him to come home at an appropriate time from his trips because on the very next trip he had his secretary book his flight home on a Saturday evening. When I asked him why he was ignoring my request, he said his secretary made the flight arrangements. I was angry during his weeklong trip and into the following week. That Friday evening, I had to go to the grocery store because there was very little food in the pantry and refrigerator. I was very tired and still angry but tried my best to put on a happy face for Casey. I asked her to go to the grocery store with me. We quickly did our shopping and came home around 7:00 P.M. Melvin was sitting in his reclining chair, watching television with not a care in the world. Somehow this got me so angry. I yelled at him and said, "You could have made an attempt to make yourself useful even if it was just to set the table." He looked at me calmly and said, "You know I don't like to argue." He continued watching television.

I felt like I was being taken advantage of, and I also was beginning to feel like a doormat. I decided that we needed to seriously think about our marriage and that one of us should move out of the house. So I decided he should have the honor of moving out since he refused to change his traveling habits. That evening I asked him to leave our home, which he did without hesitation. The next day, he called and wanted to know how Casey and I were doing. He also said it was silly and childish for me to get so angry about his trips. My asking him to leave probably ended our marriage because he made my life miserable for the next several months. He said he would continue to return home from his travels on Saturday or Sunday and that I should accept it. This gave a strong indication our marriage was ending, but I still had hopes that we could come to some amicable agreement.

My once loving, patient, and easygoing husband became very hostile for the next several months. I never knew he could be so hateful and mean until we separated. He became like a chameleon. When he was not being hateful, he would call me at the office as though everything was fine between us. During these horrible months, I knew I had made a good decision on asking him to leave our home. It was also evident that I needed to move on with my life. So I made a decision to move on and concentrate solely on my career and raising my daughter.

One morning he called me at the office while I was fixing coffee for everyone. The rule in our office was to have the person who arrived first to fix the coffee. Well, I heard my telephone ring as I turned on the coffee machine, so I ran to get it, unaware that I was still holding the coffee pot. It was Melvin, calling just to chat. While he was talking to me, I heard my supervisor ask what happened. I realized I still had the coffee pot in my hand. I hung up the phone quickly and ran back to the coffee machine to find coffee running onto the floor.

While cleaning up the mess, I heard my phone ringing again, but I did not answer it. When I got back to my desk, my phone started ringing again. It was Melvin again, and he said in a very harsh tone, "You better not ever hang up on me again or you will be sorry." I was so shocked that I did not respond to his mean statement. Instead, I explained what happened with the coffee pot. He found this to be very funny and started laughing—a laugh that sounded like he was ridiculing me.

He never came home and never apologized for anything. I, on the other hand, apologized for asking him to leave and tried to mend our marriage. I got us a marriage counselor and asked him if he was willing to come with me. He agreed to attend a session with me, but it did not work out the way I had anticipated. Our first session ended with him getting angry and leaving within the first ten minutes of our counseling session. I stopped all future sessions that evening.

Many things happened over the next several months. He did not want a divorce but wanted to think about our situation for a while. This did not make sense to me because one evening he called me at home and said he did not love me or want me anymore. I asked him why, then, he was prolonging our marriage, but he could not give me a good answer. This man, who no longer loved or wanted me, would call me all the time to chat about nonsensical things. He also took me to dinner on several occasions. Today, I would never entertain such bizarre behavior since it just encourages a spiteful spouse to impose hurtful and unnecessary mental anguish on you.

Shortly after telling me he no longer loved or wanted me, he called one morning around 4:00 A.M., asking me to bail him out of jail. Like a fool, I felt sorry for him and bailed him out the next morning. This type of behavior was definitely not from the man I married. Apparently, he visited a nightclub the previous evening and, fool that he was, attempted to drive home while intoxicated. A few blocks from his home, he was pulled over by a police car, given a breath test, and then hauled into jail with a positive result. His car was towed and impounded. Devastated by the charge, Melvin feared losing his driver's license and serving more jail time. Like a fool, I came to his rescue and located an attorney, who pulled off a decent defense. Avoiding jail time by virtue of this being his first offense, Melvin managed to hang on to his license. He never drank after that. The scare was enough for him.

Shortly after this incident, I had a serious talk with him on the status of our marriage at one of the beautiful recreation parks in Washington. Unfortunately, he did not want to discuss it or make any decisions. The day of our discussion, I told him I no longer wanted to try keeping our marriage intact and wanted to move forward on divorce proceedings. I also told him that he would be responsible for the cost, and I left him sitting there.

Many times during our separation, I felt my heart would break. I had failed in matrimony, again. That was how it felt like to me. Really, though, matrimony had failed me. One thing that made me happy was that Melvin kept in constant touch with his daughter, Casey. He would take her to dinner when she was not too busy with school. Casey was now attending a local university. She was accepted to an Ivy League school but decided to stay close to home. I begged her to go, but she did not want me to be alone and wanted to stay close to home. So she applied and attended a local university.

After discussing my desire to move forward with the divorce proceedings, as the saying goes, "I picked myself up and dusted myself off." I started working twice as hard in my job. I put my full concentration on my career and Casey, who had grown into a beautiful young woman. In addition to attending college, she worked part time at one of the intelligence agencies. She was happy and still loved her father, Melvin. Even though she was grown and mature far beyond her age, I still wanted to make sure she was taken care of while still living under my roof. Melvin finally agreed to end our marriage after two years of separation. We worked out the divorce details together and parted ways with no harsh feelings. He was diagnosed with lymphoma and passed away two years after our divorce. When he got sick, Casey and I thought he would recover because he was in excellent health and had never been ill in his life. However, the disease took his life within six months. The death of her father was so devastating that she cried for days. Casey and I will always remember the wonderful times we had together as a family.

I reminded myself that I was not totally responsible for my failed marriages and I should not feel like a loser. I also reminded myself that I helped both husbands financially, stood by them, and encouraged them to reach their dreams. I threw myself into my work at NASA and also started looking for a higher-level position in other federal agencies. As Mr. Burston had told me long ago, I was not a bureaucrat and should change jobs every two to three years. This was another excellent piece of advice I received from him, and I followed this advice then and for the rest of my career.

The incident on board the space shuttle *Challenger* in 1986 served as a tragic reminder of the realities of space exploration. I narrowly missed watching the explosion on television when, while at the Goddard Center on January 28, 1986, I had got caught up with work at my desk, missing the launch. Running down the hall to try to catch some footage, I was met by one of the engineers. He looked devastated. Apparently, the space shuttle blew apart a few seconds into its flight, killing all seven crewmembers on board. Christa McAuliffe, the first member of the Teacher in Space Project, was one of the seven killed that day. This was my last day at NASA and a day for obvious reasons I shall not forget, but it was time to move on. I had accepted a job offer from the Internal Revenue (IRS) in Washington, D.C., and it seemed too good to pass up.

## Chapter 31

The job at the IRS was to serve as one of two section chiefs in the newly created Information Technology Division. IRS is sometimes referred to as the tax collection agency. My job at the IRS elevated my government grade system back to the pay scale I was at when I was terminated by the Department of Energy. The IRS, during this period, was in the process of hiring qualified senior-level people to help establish a good federal acquisition system. This meant the door was wide open for establishing sound and workable federal acquisition policies and procedures. I was very excited to be hired because I now had a lot of experience in the field of federal acquisitions, and I knew the rules and regulations like my right hand.

I had both women and men on my staff at IRS who needed a lot of training and hand holding in the field of federal acquisitions. The job required developing, negotiating, awarding, and implementing federal contracts for the supplies and services needed by the federal government. I quickly found out that almost everyone in the IRS did not know the federal statutes and rules and regulations that provided the necessary instructions and guidance on acquiring supplies and services for the federal government. When, and if, they did, many employees, including upper management, did not believe it was necessary to follow them.

One month into the job, I found it essential to send a Cure Notice to a contractor whose performance was less than satisfactory and who had fallen far behind the contract completion date. A Cure Notice within the federal government acquisition system is a written notice that informs the contractor that it has failed to perform its contractual obligations in accordance with the terms and conditions of the contract. The contractor is given a certain period of time to carry out its obligations, and failure to do so will often lead to termination of the contract.

The notice I issued to the contractor did not win me any brownie points, and my new supervisor turned the other way and left me twisting in the wind. Two days after I sent the notice, I received a call from one of the special assistants to the Cabinet Secretary of the Treasury. IRS is under the jurisdiction of the Department of Treasury. The assistant said the Office of the Secretary received a call from the president of the company and had faxed a copy of my letter to him.

The special assistant wanted to know why this letter was sent even though the reason for the notice was included in the three-page letter. I explained the reasons again and provided supporting federal acquisition laws that permitted such action to be taken by the federal government. He listened for a few minutes and then said I was being arbitrary and capricious and that I could be dismissed from my position. He also said that some employees had been terminated from their positions for lesser actions. I was told I would be receiving a call from the Office of the Commissioner of IRS within the next few minutes. The special assistant sounded very angry, and I could hear him slamming the telephone down on the receiver.

I was on my own and had no one to ask for help. I became anxious and thought maybe my career was over. As the special assistant had said, I received a call from one of the senior staff members from the commissioner's office. It was a woman who I later discovered was an attorney. Once again, I told my story, and to my surprise, she said she would set up a meeting immediately to reach some kind of resolution. She called me an hour later and said for me to come to the conference room next to the commissioner's office on the fifth floor of the building.

When I arrived at the meeting, there sat my supervisor, the director of the Federal Acquisition Policy Office, director of the Federal Acquisition Operations office, two men from the Office of the Cabinet Secretary of the Treasury, three men from the commissioner's office, and the woman who called me earlier. I was ready to answer any and all questions and also ready for the worst as far as my career was concerned. During my early career years, I realized I worked very well under stress and stormy situations. However, this was more than a stressful and stormy situation; I felt like I was facing the firing squad. When I noticed there were only two women in the room, I had an adrenaline rush, causing my heart rate to skyrocket. I was one of the two women and the only minority in the room.

The woman who called me turned out to be one of the attorneys within the Department of Treasury. She got up and explained what transpired between the contractor, the Department of Treasury, and the commissioner's office. After she gave the sequence of events, she turned it over to me to tell my story. I explained that the contractor was deficient in the performance of the contract and the contract was one year behind schedule. I went on to say the contractor was still being paid despite poor performance and that no government representative was assigned to monitor the contract.

## The Forgotten American

During my briefing, I cited the appropriate statutes and rules and regulations that supported the action I took. When I finished, my supervisor tried to explain why the contractor was behind and why he was still getting paid, but the attorney who set up the meeting stopped him and took over the conversation. She wanted my supervisor and me to meet with the contractor to set some timetables to bring the contract back on schedule and to correct all the deficiencies identified in my letter. She also recommended that all payments be stopped until the contract was modified to include all corrective actions to be taken and signed by IRS and the contractor.

I met with the contractor the next day, and we had a successful meeting. We established some ground rules and modified the contract. With a lot of hand holding, to my delight, the contractor did get the contract back on schedule and was near completion when I left the program. In the end, everyone who got involved in this case said they learned a lot but never said, "Thank you for leading us in the right direction," or "Thank you for saving the contract." They never do trust me.

Throughout my career, I found too many people working outside the field of federal acquisitions, ready to fight the decisions I made. Afterward, when they realized they could not get away with even half of what they were trying to pull off, comments such as, "I learned a lot," flew like confetti at a wedding. Nobody ever said thank you, but perhaps this will change one day.

The first six months of my job at the IRS were more than challenging. My supervisor and I had many heated discussions because he did not know the federal laws and rules and regulations that govern the expenditure of the public's tax dollars. It was not easy to work for him. It took a lot of time and energy to convince him there were laws, rules, and regulations that all federal agencies must follow. After working with him for six months, he finally went to a two-week basic federal acquisition-training course. When he returned, he admitted he did not know much and that he learned a lot during the two-week session. It was a little more pleasant to work with him after this training session.

After a year and half with the Information Technology Division, the director of the Federal Acquisition Policy Office asked me if I was interested in joining his staff. He wanted employees who were well versed in law and federal acquisitions to write policies for the IRS Federal Acquisition Department. He had received approval to add two new senior-level positions and wanted to fill them as quickly as possible. I was very interested, so I applied and was selected for one of the policy positions.

My life in the Federal Acquisition Policy Division gave me even more authority than my previous job in the Information Technology Division. In this office, I was not only responsible for writing policies but also for reviewing federal contracts before they were awarded to various private companies. I was also responsible for training federal acquisition employees out in the field offices across the United States. Despite the workload and the constant barrage of questions from employees, both from the field and internal offices, I truly enjoyed my job until I ran into what I consider to be gender and race discrimination.

## Chapter 32

In the spring of 1989, I applied for a position as a branch chief for the small purchases branch. I was more than qualified for the job, but I did not get it. The Caucasian man selected did not have the academic credentials or the amount of experience I had in the field of federal acquisition. This discriminatory act was so obvious to me and others that I decided to do something about it. I met with the selection committee to find out the reason for not being selected, but the committee was not able to provide definitive answers as to why I was not chosen for the job.

I was not happy with the shallow and vague answers I received from the selection committee. However, I did not want to yell discrimination for not being selected and appear like a poor loser. I thought about the unsatisfactory answers I received from the selection committee before making a decision on my next step. I truly wanted to know any deficiencies going against my qualification for the position. So I filed a discrimination suit with the equal-opportunity office within the IRS. Upon a long investigation, the agency determined there was no discrimination based on gender or race and dismissed it. This certainly was not acceptable to me; therefore, I hired an attorney from the private sector.

My attorney immediately filed a discrimination suit against the IRS. Based on his findings and some discussions with the IRS, he requested the IRS afford me a hearing before an administrative law judge from the U.S. Equal Employment Opportunity Commission. The commission is an independent federal agency that enforces laws against workplace discrimination. It investigates discrimination complaints based on race, color, and national origin, religion, sex, age, and disability, as well as retaliation actions for reporting discrimination practices.

The administrative judge who was assigned to the case found there was, indeed, gender and race discrimination in the selection process. He set a hearing for all parties concerned on a Friday afternoon. My immediate supervisor, the

IRS attorney handling the case, my attorney, and I were requested to attend the hearing by the administrative judge. The administrative judge had determined that giving me monetary compensation was the appropriate action for the harm done to me. The hearing started out really well until it became very clear that the IRS attorney was not prepared and could not adequately defend the agency. Since the IRS attorney was not prepared to make an offer for the harm done to me so I could be made whole again, the judge closed the meeting. To "make whole" is a legal term used in reference to compensating a party for a loss sustained, either economic or noneconomic. The judge was so annoyed that he scolded the IRS attorney right in front of us. He requested the IRS attorney meet with the appropriate senior officials and come back to him with an appropriate monetary offer to make me whole again.

The next meeting was to take place only between the administrative judge and the IRS attorney. The judge said I would be hearing from him and the IRS once they settled the offer made by IRS. Two weeks later, I received a letter from the IRS and was sitting at the dining room table reading it when Casey came into the room and wanted to know what I was doing. I gave the letter to her to read. Upon reading it, she said, "Good grief, this sounds like the Karen Silkwood case." IRS had offered me a large sum of money to settle the case, and that was why Casey compared it to the Silkwood case.

Karen Silkwood (1946-1974) was a young chemical technician at the Kerr-McGee plant near Crescent, Oklahoma. Her job was to make plutonium pellets for nuclear reactor fuel rods. She was an American labor union activist who investigated and documented claims of safety violations at the plant. She was on her way to hand-deliver her findings to a New York reporter when she died in a one-car crash outside of Crescent. Her findings were never found at the crash scene. Antinuclear activists view her as a martyr, and her story was made into a film, *Silkwood,* in 1983. Casey and I saw the movie, and she remembered Karen Silkwood being offered a large sum of money to keep quiet, and that was why she compared my case to that story.

I explained to Casey the IRS made me a monetary offer because I was harmed by the agency and they wanted to make restitution. I further explained to her they could never make me whole again, but I was ready to take the money since I was planning to move on to another agency. I told Casey that I was asked by a former colleague to apply for a position within the agency where he worked and I would be applying for a position there. I told her I wanted to follow the good advice of Mr. Burston, who had long ago advised me to work only two or three years at each agency.

My working days at the IRS were filled with many challenging hours, but I would, on occasion, have a chance to wind down and have a laugh. I had a young male staff member by the name of Jack, who would play tricks on me when he saw I was totally stressed out.

## The Forgotten American

One late afternoon, I came back from a long meeting with upper management and found a note stuck to my telephone. The message said to call Mr. Bear immediately upon my return to the office. I had not yet put my briefcase away when Jack rushed into my office and said, "Did you call Mr. Bear yet?" He also said, "Mr. Bear wants to discuss a very important matter and wants to talk to you before you leave for the day." So I called the number several times, but it was always busy.

There was no voicemail in those days, so the telephones would just ring until one hung up. Jack kept checking to see if I reached Mr. Bear several more times. I finally got through, and a female voice answered with, "Washington National Zoo, can I help you?" At that moment, I realized the name on the note was the same as the name of the large furry animal at the zoo. I told her I must have dialed the wrong number and knew immediately that Jack was up to his tricks again. At that moment, Jack came rushing to my office again and I gave him a stern look, held up my hand, and motioned him to go away. I could hear muffled laughter from the rest of the staff. It had been a long, tedious day for me, and the joke was not funny to me at the time. It was not until I was driving home when I found the joke to be funny. I started laughing, and my whole body finally relaxed.

Jack was a very handsome young man who was always happy. After I left the IRS, one of my former staff members called and informed me that Jack had contracted AIDS and he had given his two-week termination notice to the IRS. He evidently did not have very long to live. I was told he was going on a month-long vacation to Europe with a friend. My former staff member recommended I wait to call him when he returned from his vacation and that someone would call me upon his return. I never got to call him because the next call was to tell me he had died, and the funeral was the next day. I did not ask anyone how he contracted AIDS. I just wanted to remember his happy face and him as a good-natured man who worked hard every day.

## Chapter 33

I decided it was time to leave the IRS and seek new opportunities in another federal agency as soon as I settled my discrimination suit. Mark, a former IRS colleague, had previously been selected for a position at the Federal Aviation Administration (FAA). He called, giving me "heads up" regarding various job openings during the processing of my discrimination case. FAA is an agency within the Department of Transportation with the authority to regulate and oversee all aspects of civil aviation in the U.S. Mark said the FAA needed experienced senior-level employees with accounting and law backgrounds. I told him that I could not leave but would give it serious consideration when my discrimination case was settled.

As soon as I settled my discrimination suit, I contacted Mark and told him I was ready to apply for any senior-level position in the FAA. He sent me several vacancy announcements, and I applied for all of the positions. I was selected for a team leader position in one of the acquisition offices, which I accepted wholeheartedly.

I was in the team leader position for less than a year when I applied for an associate program manager position within the same office that was responsible for the development and award of FAA's communication, aircraft, and weather systems. Upon my selection, the division director of that office had a meeting with me, and the first thing he said was, "This office is in bad shape, and I need your help in cleaning it up and getting it back on the right track. You and I inherited one of the worst offices in the agency." He went on to say the office consisted of incompetent and ill-trained employees. He wished me good luck and said, "I know you can do it." I was glad he told me the whole truth.

Once on the job, I found out the office was worse than what the director had told me. Work had piled up on everyone's desk, and not one employee could give me an acceptable briefing on the status of the project he or she was working on.

I went through each project with each of the staff members and prioritized his or her workload. One staff member got angry when I told her which project had the highest priority. She got up and started walking toward the door in a huff. I told her in a very firm tone to come back and sit down until I finished with my instructions. I did not know whether she would come back or continue walking out, but fortunately for me, she came back and listened. After our little spat, she became very cooperative and stayed with me and worked hard until I left that agency.

I did a lot of hands-on training for the next six months. I also encouraged and helped two men under my supervision to find jobs in other agencies where the work was less demanding. They wanted to leave because of the heavy workload within our office. They also did not want to work under my supervisor, who was considered to be a very hard-driving and demanding man. It was evident these two men needed more experience and training for the type of work our office was required to perform. I encouraged them to find jobs in a smaller agency where the work was not so demanding. Within a few months, both men found jobs. Six months after they left, I found out they were doing very well in the agencies they joined.

I was asked by one of the directors from IRS a couple of years later to provide a briefing on work performance for one of these men. He had applied to IRS for a senior-level position in the finance department and had listed me as his former supervisor. After providing the necessary information to IRS, I recommended him for the job, since I knew his performance was now at the outstanding level. He was selected for the job, and his supervisor told me several months later that he was doing an excellent job for them and thanked me for recommending him. This shows that proper guidance and faith in your fellow employees will get them on the right path to success.

I worked tirelessly for the next six months training my staff on federal acquisition laws, rules, and regulations, and helping them to get back on schedule with their projects. During this period, I was given approval to add one more position to my staff, which was advertised by our personnel office. When I started my work in this office, my supervisor told me to keep a racially balanced staff. Although my staff was pretty close to being racially balanced, I selected a minority woman from the list of eligible applicants. My selection of Johanna from the list of eligible applicants did not turn out well. Sending her to formal training courses along with my day-to-day personal training did not help much, either. Although I was very tired of continuously correcting her work, I never gave up on her. But one evening, just before I was ready to go home, my supervisor called me into his office. He informed me that my staff and projects were being transferred to another person and that Johanna would now be working for another colleague of mine. I asked why, but he did not want to discuss it and just said his decision was best for everyone. Right there and then, I figured it was Johanna who was behind this bad scenario. I did not ask any more questions and just left for home immediately.

I was very angry and knew it was best not to discuss anything when in that state of mind. I seethed with anger all the way home. My staff, once viewed by my supervisor as incompetent and ill trained, was now well trained and had become competent in their assigned areas. The bad projects were back on schedule with many completed all because of my tireless effort. I worked anywhere from ten to fifteen hours a day, six or sometimes seven days a week, bringing this office back to normalcy. I thought of the Best of the Best Award I received from the agency that year, which eased my pain a little. But this latest action was truly painful and degrading. I concluded that my supervisor and managers above him no longer needed my services now that the program I inherited was in excellent shape.

I decided it was time to leave. I had overstayed the years of service that Mr. Burston had recommended to me. I made excuses by telling myself that I was still within the two-to-three-year range that he had recommended because I served in two different offices. But I knew it was indeed time to leave. I had no regrets for the decision to leave since I had accomplished a lot for the agency. In addition, the bureaucracy was beginning to gnaw at my stomach. I also knew I had to move away from my present office, while seeking a new job in another agency.

The next morning, I met with another director in another office who was searching for an employee to fill a vacant position. He said it was only a staff position, but if I did not mind, he would be glad to have me detailed to his office for ninety days. I was very happy that he immediately met with the appropriate officials, and within two days, I was approved for a detail to this office.

The first evening of my new position, I decided to stay late to review some contracts when my former demanding supervisor rushed into my new office. His eyes were bulging and his face was red with anger. He demanded me to move all my books and supplies out of my old office that evening. I told him I was planning to do it in the morning since I was about ready to leave for the evening. He wanted it done that evening. As he was leaving, he said that even though higher management approved my detail to another office, he was still my supervisor. I knew then I had to speed up my search for a new job.

I made this arrogant individual look good in the eyes of higher management by working tirelessly to clean up one of the worst run offices with the FAA. However, he no longer saw me as an asset, based on the whining of one of my staff members, who I am sure felt she was being picked on without cause. Despite my day-to-day tutelage, this woman made little effort to learn and grasp the necessary rules and regulations surrounding the work she was required to do. Later on I learned the woman and my manager viewed my tutelage as harassment. A good manager would have gotten the story from both parties to reach a resolution. It was more than disappointing that he did not even ask to hear my side of the story when he met with me. During this difficult time, I remembered Mr. Burston telling me, "My best advice for having a bad supervisor is to seek other employment as soon as possible, and never undervalue your happiness."

I knew if I fought long and hard enough, I could win the battle on getting my position back, but I had become very tired of the bureaucracy. Even if I won the battle, there was no guarantee that I would be happy in the changed environment. It is always wise to think through any difficult situation and to choose wisely which battle is worth fighting.

I decided that night I would search for a new job and planned to leave before my detail of ninety days was up. Within one week of starting my detail in the new office, I asked for an official transfer to the new office, which was accepted that same week. I knew I had made the right decision and was very happy to know the authoritarian man was no longer my supervisor. Being happy was important to me because it goes hand in hand with good performance.

## Chapter 34

One evening after working on my resume for a new job, I could not get to sleep, so I just tossed and turned for a while. Instead of falling asleep, I started thinking about the many difficult paths I had traveled and hard decisions I had to make while working at FAA. I had managed to put the worst managed office back to an exceptional rating, and that was good. In order to get the office back on track, I rolled up my sleeves and assisted my staff with their projects. In addition to working along with them, I provided hands-on training to them on a daily basis. One thing I did not do, like many managers today, was to sit in my office and look important.

I thought back to the first week I took over as an associate program manager, when I received a contractor's claim for $25,000. The allegation from the company was that it was for interest earned on late payments from the federal agency. I did not assign it to any of the staff members but took on the task myself. After weeks of researching and coordinating my efforts with the manager of the accounting and financial office, I concluded the contractor was owed only $2,000. As the authorized representative of the federal government with an unlimited warrant to make decisions, I prepared a letter outlining the reason for my decision. Upon review by our agency contracts attorney, I sent it to the president of the company. In this decision memorandum, I informed him this was my final decision and the organization could appeal it to the agency's Board of Contract Appeals or bring action directly in the U.S. Claims Court. The contractor did not appeal my decision.

One week later, I received another claim for the amount of $6.7 million from a systems development contractor. Based on my research and consultation with the agency finance office, I denied the claim in its entirety. Again I informed the contractor this was my final decision and the company could appeal it to the agency's Board of Contract Appeals or bring action directly in the U.S. Claims

Court. The contractor contested my decision before the Board of Contract Appeals. Upon receipt of the company's appeal, the Board of Contract Appeals directed the contractor to submit clear and compelling justification for its claim. The company requested additional time, and we did not hear from it for quite some time.

Many months later, our contracts attorney met with me in my office and said the company wanted to settle and was withdrawing its appeal. He said the company presented a counter proposal for a $75,000 settlement. I told him its proposal was not acceptable and it still had time to submit the justification that was requested by the Board of Contract Appeals.

The attorney said, "Paula, you and I have spent about $100,000 worth of our time on this claim, and we will most likely spend another $50,000 if we do not accept their counter proposal. If we settle now, we come out ahead by paying only the $75,000." I told him I would think about it overnight and get back to him in the morning. I left him standing there with a look of surprise.

As I promised the attorney, I thought very hard about the offer of $75,000 that night. After agonizing over the company's counter offer, I determined the attorney was correct; we would spend more money if the company appealed my decision. However, I did not believe $75,000 was the appropriate amount for settling the claim. After running some numbers, I decided to settle for a total of $60,000 instead of $75,000.

The next morning, I informed the attorney that $60,000 was the appropriate amount to settle the claim. The attorney informed me later that day that he discussed our offer of $60,000, and the president accepted it. I was glad it was finally settled, but what bothered me was the initial claim of $6.7 million. If a thorough research had not been performed, the contractor just might have received the $6.7 million to which he believed he was entitled.

Throughout my career, I always performed thorough research on all subject matters at issue before making any final decisions. I know I was hard on contractors and my staff members, but I made sure I was fair in my judgments and decisions. I once overheard a couple of my staff members refer to me as "strict but always fair" when asked by some engineers how it was to work for me. Looking back on my career, I was indeed hard my on my staff, but I wanted them to learn and move on to higher and better positions. I always told my employees they should not only work hard but also learn as much as they could under my supervision. I always encouraged them to seek new opportunities when they believed they were ready.

That night, still not able to sleep, my mind wandered onto two very sad occasions. Within one year of my tenure at FAA, two of my staff members died while on vacation. One staff member by the name of Agnes died while whitewater rafting in West Virginia one weekend. When I was selected as the associate program manager, she requested to be transferred from another office to my office. She was a young mother who already had a couple of grandchildren. She was a very hardworking woman and always in a pleasant mood.

## The Forgotten American

While flying on United Airlines to our Oklahoma City field office one spring morning, I sensed something was wrong and told myself that I should call my office from the airport. The airport was very busy, and I did not want to waste time, so I got my rental car and proceeded to the field office. Upon my arrival, I was met in the hallway by one of the field directors. He had a very somber look. I knew immediately that something was wrong, but I thought it was work related. He said, "Your staff members have called several times and are anxious to talk with you." He went on to say, "I am sorry to hear about one of your staff members passing away over the weekend." He then ushered me to an empty office for me to call back to my office.

Agnes had told me before she left on vacation that her husband and some friends were going on a whitewater rafting trip while on vacation. She had accompanied her husband and friends on a whitewater-rafting trip that weekend in West Virginia. Evidently their rafting boat hit a very large current, and she fell overboard. After many attempts by the rescue crew to find her body, the water was turned off that afternoon to make it easier to search, but they still were not able to find her body. The rescue crew did not find her body until the next evening. She was discovered under a big boulder near the place where she fell off the boat. Although she had a lifejacket on, it is believed she hit her head on the boulder and died instantly and was sucked beneath by the fierce currents.

Nine months later Patricia another staff member died while on vacation in the Bahamas. Prior to leaving for her time off, I asked her if she had her yearly physical exam and any shots necessary for going to the Bahamas. She had taken care of everything, so I told her to enjoy her two-week trip with her niece and sister. At the end of her vacation period, she was to accompany me to assist with the negotiation sessions I had scheduled with an engineering company in Melbourne, Florida. Her cruise ship was scheduled to dock on Sunday afternoon at Port Canaveral, located in Cape Canaveral about fourteen miles from Melbourne. She was to meet my two pricing specialists and me that Sunday evening at the hotel where we all had reservations.

That Sunday night, I stayed up until midnight for a call from her. I also checked the hotel front desk to see if she checked in, but she never showed up that Sunday evening. The next morning, I became very worried, so I called back to my office and asked Joanie, one of the staff members, to call our personnel office. She was to let them know Patricia was missing and to get a number for a family member from them. I asked her to call the family member to find out if they had heard from Patricia. I also asked Joanie not to say anything to anyone in the office until we located Patricia. While waiting for Patricia to show up at the hotel, I remembered that I sensed something was wrong when I arrived at the Orlando airport, where I was to rent a car and drive down to Melbourne. I did not know whether it was related to my negotiation sessions or to something else. I always checked on my daughter when I had these strange feelings, so I called my daughter to make sure everything was fine with her. She was fine and told me not to worry about anything.

On Monday morning, we met with about fifteen employees from the engineering company. After the introduction of my team, I informed the group that Patricia was also scheduled to attend the session and most likely would be arriving later in the morning. We proceeded with negotiations, and twenty minutes into our session, I was told I had an emergency call. I knew right then that something terrible had happened to Patricia. I was ushered into a private room, where the phone was blinking for pickup. I picked up the phone, and all I could hear was crying at the other end. Joanie, whom I had asked to find Patricia, finally got control of her crying to tell me her findings. She said that Patricia had passed away on the beach in the Bahamas on Saturday.

Later that day, we found out that she died of congestive heart failure. I was so shocked and saddened and wanted to stop negotiations and go home that day. However, I knew Patricia would have wanted us to complete negotiations before going home. After informing everyone in the negotiations session about Patricia's death, we took a short break and then proceeded with the session. Patricia was another staff member who was a very kind woman, always happy and willing to learn new ways of doing business. She never seemed to have a bad day.

I was so sad about losing two staff members in less than a year that I began to wonder if my supervision had something to do with their deaths. One day my supervisor, with whom I was still in good graces, called me into his office to assure me that their deaths had nothing to do with my supervision. He said, "You did more than anyone in the agency to help them, and they were grateful for your help and guidance." This eased my sadness a little, but it took me many months to get over their passing.

These two women were very kind, considerate, and friendly, and I often wonder why people like them are always taken from us in their early years. My mother was the most generous and kindhearted of all her eight brothers and sisters, yet she died while still fairly young. Her brothers and sisters are still living except for one brother, who died at the age of seventy-five. One colleague told me the reason they are taken from us early in their lives is because they have completed their mission on earth. It may be selfish, but I believe these types of people should be the ones to remain on earth so they can be examples of what a good human being should be like.

## Chapter 35

Up to now, I had never been accused of abusing my authority while serving as a representative of the federal government. I stopped a negotiation session for a $10-million claim and several weeks later, the engineering company from Florida sent a searing letter to the agency's assistant secretary for administration. According to the letter, I had abused my power of authority as an associate program manager. The letter further stated that the contracting officer's warrant held by me did not give me complete authority to make decisions for the government.

This was one of the most difficult and tiring negotiations sessions I had held with a large engineering company in Melbourne. It was a very complicated claimed I tackled myself. After weeks of research and consultation with my engineers, I found the FAA did not owe the company the amount they submitted. After establishing a negotiation position far below the asking price, I set up a negotiation session with the engineering company. I requested the session be held at the company's office in Melbourne, and the company agreed to the arrangement.

The negotiation session did not start out very well. The engineering company had just hired a new manager for their contracting office. She was very combative and immediately created a hostile environment. She wandered away from the main negotiation issue time after time. The head of its engineering team, although very well versed in our contract with them, also became combative within an hour of our session. On the morning of the second day, he became very angry. Grabbing his briefcase and muttering, he left the room. I continued the negotiation session without blinking an eye. One of their engineering team members asked if we could stop the session until he returned. I calmly said, "Absolutely not. If he is truly interested in settling the claim, he will return." I also said that he if he did not return, I would close the negotiation session, and we could all go home. He did return to our session after lunch and apologized for his nasty behavior.

## Paula B. Compton

After negotiating for four straight days, both parties had successfully settled only one of twenty items of the claim. On the fourth day, the manager and head engineer became even more aggressive and combative. At lunch that day, I told my team that if the session continued as it did all week, I would be making a final decision on the amount to be paid by the federal agency and close the session. Everyone thought it was the only fair thing to do since the company could not provide substantive information to support its claim.

In typical fashion, the afternoon session got off to a very bad start when the manager of its contracting office started accusing us of lying and causing their company to perform additional work that was not written in the contract. By this time, I had enough of her negative and combative behavior. She had set the negative tone for her team on day one of our negotiation session, and they all followed suit. When you are in a lead position, it is very important to set a positive and invigorating tone in order to establish a positive working environment.

I did not want to go back to Washington without settling the claim, but I knew it was necessary in this case. I stood up and informed everyone that because we had made very little progress in the four days of negotiation, I was closing negotiations and making a contracting officer's final decision. I further stated that because the corporation was not able to provide substantive information to support its claim, my final decision was for the amount of $4 million.

I informed the negotiation participants that my final decision was based on thorough research in consultation with the federal agency's engineering team. I further stated the company could appeal my decision and I would provide the appeal process in writing upon my return to Washington. Excusing my team, I concluded my portion of the meeting. The head of the engineering company asked the members of his team to remain and asked me when I would be sending the letter. I told him I would fax a copy on Monday morning, and Federal Express would send the original. Shortly after this nasty negotiation session, I left the agency for greener pastures at another federal agency.

The news of my final decision got back to Washington before I even boarded the plane. Upon my return, my manager and I were requested to meet with the agency's associate administrator for administration and her two special assistants. I was asked to provide a briefing on my decision, which I did with briefing charts summarizing the facts of the case. On my flight back to Washington, I prepared my briefing charts since I suspected I would be requested to brief senior management. Before I could even complete my briefing, the two special assistants started throwing questions at me left and right. I was not about to be outdone, so I started throwing answers back just as quickly. After thirty minutes of the chaos, the race was over. The associate director thanked me for an excellent job and said they would support my final decision. I don't like to lose, and rarely do I lose in cases like this, so I was delighted to come out as the winner.

Nine months after I left the agency, I received several calls from former colleagues who were more than eager to tell me the engineering company was paid in full for the claim. They told me the engineering company's contract was modified for payment of the full amount of the claim that I had denied. Megan, who was assigned to administer this contract and who did not have the training or experience to handle multi-million-dollar contracts, called me that same day. She was very upset and wanted to meet with me. She said her supervisor (my former supervisor), who had taken away my staff and projects over a year ago, was in the process of firing her. Evidently, the combative woman manager from the engineering company in Florida talked Megan into paying the $10-million claim. Without reviewing and researching the history, she modified the contract and paid the company the full amount of the original claim.

    I met with Megan over lunch the day after she called. She gave me the details and reasons for the actions she took on the claim. I then gave her some guidance on steps she needed to take now that the damage was done. I assured her the agency most likely would not fire her. I also told her it would not be in the best interest of the agency to fire her for this incident and that her supervisor, including his manager, was at fault as well. Megan did not get fired, and the agency got their money back. I understand it was finally settled through the dispute resolution method. In the end, the engineering company made off with a little over the $4 million I authorized; however, at the end of the day, it was a lot less than the original ten.

    During our meeting, Megan told me that my staff and projects were disbursed among several section chiefs within the division I once worked. I found this to be so unfair and disgusting. I had been expected to carry a large workload that included many multi-million-dollar projects. Like some private organizations, but more so in the federal government, the more competent one is, the more work one gets. When I started my career, I discovered very quickly that senior management normally did not delegate much work to people who were considered to be either incompetent or those treated as the "favorite son" of the organization. Anyone with good managerial skills would never allow such nonsense; unfortunately, many people in management positions lack good management skills.

    In the early days of my career, I remember saying to one of my colleagues that it would be nice not to have so much work. She gave me a serious look and said, "Paula, you would never be happy in a job like that, and your conscience would never allow you to settle for mediocre work." She is right; having been raised with strong work ethics and having a type-A personality, I could never permit myself to perform poorly on the job. According to psychologists, people with type-A personalities are competitive, driven, stressed, and workaholics. They are strict and rigid and are perfectionist types of people.

## Chapter 36

My beautiful daughter, Casey, had now received her bachelor's and master's degrees and had entered the workforce. She had been selected to serve abroad by the intelligence agency she had previously worked for during her college years. Her training program was vigorous with a view to a diplomatic assignment abroad. I had always told her that I would give her full support in any career she chose. I was comfortable with all her training activities except for the last training assignment.

One evening toward the end of her training program, she met me at the top of the stairwell when I arrived home from work. She showed me her combat boots and fatigue clothing for the final stint of her training. She was very excited about this particular assignment. I was shocked and mortified to see such clothing but tried not to show my feelings. I calmly said I wanted to hear about her last adventure, especially the location where the training was to take place. When she finished, I became very worried. However, I told her I was happy for her since I had promised her long ago that I would give her my full support in her chosen field of work.

After completing several months of training at Camp Perry, a facility used by the Department of Defense and Intelligence community, Casey told me about all the training exercises she had gone through. Based on her description of learning to shoot, and drive through hostile demonstrations, I could only assume she had experienced some sort of paramilitary training program. She refused to go into too much detail and ultimately kept the name of the program from me. The climax of this training program was to wear combat boots and fatigue clothing and trek by groups of three through wooded land and swamps all night at the training facility. Casey said it was tiresome but quite an experience to walk all night and see the dawn approach the next day. This certainly sounded like a rough and tough kind of training, but she completed it without any problems.

While waiting for her assignment abroad, she was given a short assignment with the U.S. Embassy in Vienna, Austria. A few days before she was to leave, her maternal grandfather died, which devastated her. Her grandfather and she had communicated on a regular basis since her high school days. Because he was getting up in age, we went to visit him in New Mexico when she received her master's degree. He was so proud of her but expected much more from her and requested that she get her Ph.D. soon. I had warned her that no matter how much she accomplished her grandfather would always expect her to do more, just as he did with his children. After some discussion on her grandfather's funeral, we decided it was best for her to go to Vienna as scheduled. We both left from Dulles Airport that week, she to Austria and I to New Mexico.

While Casey was in Vienna, she asked me to visit her so we could go to Italy during the weekend. This was only my third trip outside the U.S., but I had never been to Europe, so I was very excited about the trip. That long weekend with her was exhausting but exciting and fun. We took the evening train from Vienna to Venice, Italy, and arrived early in the morning in the city of canals and islands. We did not see much during our night train ride, but as morning approached we could see beautiful mountains. I was so happy to be with my beautiful and successful daughter in this great city.

Venice is filled with interesting, friendly, and hardworking people. Since cars or trucks are not allowed in the city, it makes for a perfect place to simply walk around and absorb the city's vast history. While strolling around, we saw artisans hammering out shoes, cooks whipping up wonderful-smelling dishes on hotplates, and musicians playing beautiful music in various courtyards. The back-alley galleries and artisan showrooms were full of beautiful artwork. We visited Venice's grand square, called the Piazza San Marco; the Canal Grande, which is Venice's main street; the famous Rialto Bridge; and one of the main churches along the Grand Canal called Santa Maria Della Salute. And of course, we shopped and ate at some of the best restaurants that served real Italian food. We made sure we ate at the pricey and famous restaurant called Harry's Bar, where Ernest Hemingway was a regular from the late 1940s forward. The restaurant, located on the St. Mark's Bay waterfront, was opened in 1931. It has always been a hangout and haven for Americans.

From Venice we traveled back to Salzburg, a city in west-central Austria near the German border, southwest of Linz, Italy. Wolfgang Mozart was born there in 1756, and the city hosts an annual music festival in his honor. Salzburg is an "old town" and is noted for its world-famous baroque architecture. It is also one of the best-preserved city centers in the German-speaking world.

On my last day in Vienna, I went on a tour alone since Casey had to go back to work. I did a quick city tour in the morning and spent the entire afternoon touring the beautiful Hofburg Imperial Palace, commonly known as the Winter Palace. It is the official residence of the president of Austria. This beautiful palace has six museums, a chapel dating back to the thirteenth century, a national library, a riding school, a greenhouse with incredible flora such as Alpine carnations and roses and fruit trees, and a park. The grounds of the place are huge, and one needs a full day to see all the attractions, which I was not able to do in half a day. The Lippizan horses performed at the Winter Riding School in the Winter Palace the morning I toured the area. It was amazing to watch the horses and their riders perform to classical music. These gorgeous white horses walked, trotted, and cantered to the music, in an amazing display of dressage. In all, these gray stallions performed ballet to music as though on air.

Shortly after returning from Austria, Casey was sent abroad to her real assignment for the next three years. On her final day at home, she told me this would be her last day to live with me. She said it was time to live on her own and thanked me for all the assistance I provided through the years. She said that upon her return to the U.S., she would get her own place to live. I saw her off at the airport the next day, and she was so excited about working abroad. I watched my daughter's departure, her erect frame slicing a determined path toward the future. In that singular moment, I had never been more alone. As inextricably linked with my past, she was also our future. From this moment, I would live more through her than myself. I had to let her go. As usual and like all mothers, I was very worried and concerned about her safety. I missed her so much that I did not eat very much for a whole week.

Her training at Camp Perry was put to use three weeks after she started working abroad. She was taking a friend to the airport when a motorcycle policeman stopped her. The policeman stopped her because she did not have her diplomatic license plates on her personal car. She explained that the U.S. Embassy had gotten approval from the country's appropriate officials that she could drive without the plates for the weekend. She provided her diplomat passport and U.S. Embassy papers, which authorized her to drive her personal car without the required diplomatic license plates. The embassy had given Casey its approval after receiving approval from the country's Office of Diplomatic Affairs.

The policeman said she could not drive in the city and ordered her to go to the police station, where her car was to be impounded. Since her friend had a flight to catch, she told the policeman she could not since she had to get her friend to the airport. Casey asked him to call the U.S. Marine Embassy Guards to verify the reason for her driving without diplomatic license plates. Refusing to call the guards, the officer became angrier, attracting the locals with his outburst. Picking up on the police officer's attitude and with no idea or care as to what might really be going on, they converged around the car as though ready to riot. Fearing the officer may have been employing deliberate tactics to incite a riot, Casey rolled up her window, stepped on the gas pedal, and sped away at high speed as she had been trained. The motorcycle police sped after her, and his backup blocked her up the road. At this point, she called one of the U.S. Marine Embassy Guards, who advised her to go the police station. He also asked her to speak with the angry official. After speaking with the Marine Guard, Casey was asked by the angry police officer to follow him back to the police station, where she presented her papers to the Chief of Police. After speaking with the U.S. Marine Embassy Guards, the Chief of Police apologized and allowed her to continue her trip to the airport.

She called me that evening and told me of the incident. I was fit to be tied and very concerned about the safety of my precious daughter. This was when I broke my promise of giving her my full support for any career she chose. I told her the job was not worth keeping, and I wanted her to return to the U.S. She said she wanted to think about it overnight and would get back to me the next day.

She, indeed, got back to me the next evening and said she had a job to do and was staying to complete her tour abroad. She went on to say they were not going to run her out of the country and she intended to get an official apology from the prime minister of the country. One year later, she received the official apology; however, she believes to this day that the apology was delayed deliberately because of her U.S. citizenship.

During the first month of her tour abroad and after the police incident, I made an arrangement to visit her new home. This first visit eased my concerns and worries. She was living in a gated community with guards watching the place twenty-four hours a day. It was also comforting to know that two other Americans lived in the community. During her tour abroad, we stayed in touch by telephone on a weekly basis since there was no email in those days. I visited her many times and always had such exciting and wonderful times. We visited many parts of the country where she was stationed, both tourist and non-tourist areas.

Casey and I traveled worldwide for the next twenty years, both on business and for vacation. As of this writing, we are still traveling worldwide. Many of our vacations were done together and usually around Christmas. During our travels, we visited six of the seven continents: Africa, Asia, Europe, Australia, South America, and our own North America. We have yet to visit Antarctica, the seventh continent. Some of our most interesting activities on these trips were climbing the Great Wall in China, riding camels in Egypt, crawling through tunnels in Vietnam built by the Vietnamese people during the Vietnam War, and visiting the Australian Aborigines in central Australia, including the sacred Uluru, which looks like a heart. Uluru, sacred to the Aboriginal people, is a red rock in the middle of the desert that is 1,142 feet high, 2.2 miles long, 1.2 miles wide, and 5.8 miles around. The Aboriginal people have a rich and living culture that goes back at least fifty thousand years.

Throughout our travels, we ate many native dishes such as ostrich, kangaroo, and even guinea pig—or cuy, as called in South America. I enjoyed eating kangaroo steak, which tastes like sweet filet mignon. Ostrich meat is very lean, and the taste is similar to beef. Some of the native dishes, especially the breads, were similar to traditional Native-American dishes. The people we met throughout the world learned much from us about Native Americans, and they were always delighted to meet real Native Americans. There was always much sympathy expressed by people from countries we visited concerning the genocide of Native Americans.

## Chapter 37

Shortly after my staff and projects were taken away from me at FAA, I called Ronald, an acquaintance I had known for many years, who worked at the Department of State. I told him that I wanted to get back into developing policies for the federal acquisition program. I had asked him to let me know of any positions being advertised in the Office of Policy & Review, where he worked.

He evidently did some searching within the agency before calling me during the first week of December. The Department of State, commonly referred to as the State Department, is the lead U.S. foreign affairs agency and is responsible for the international relations of the United States. I was disappointed to hear there were no vacancies in the office where he was employed. He also did not anticipate any employees leaving that office in the near future. He did alert me to an office with very few employees that was responsible for not only developing and awarding contracts but for developing federal acquisition policies. Ronald told me that because the office was responsible for only major information technology equipment, most of the work would involve developing policies. He said if I applied and was selected for the job, I would not be required to supervise any employees and I would be required to work independently and would report directly to the director of the office.

The job Ronald described sounded great, and was I ever ready to work independently and to get a break from supervising other employees. I applied for the job and within a month, I received a letter that said I had been selected for the position and was requested to confirm my acceptance of the job in writing. After confirming my acceptance of the job, I was requested to have my fingerprints taken at the FBI building and to have other necessary laboratory tests performed prior to reporting for duty.

Although my top-secret clearance for this particular field of work had just been renewed for another three years, the agency had to perform another background investigation on me for a top-secret clearance. Every federal agency is required to do a background investigation on each new employee. Each agency that employed me not only investigated my background but also had to verify my academic credentials. My type of work also required a reinvestigation of my background every three years. So once again I had to complete a questionnaire that requested everything about me from the day I was born.

I had all the security forms and test completed for the new job at the State Department before giving my two-week resignation notice to the FAA. This was in case I encountered any problems. There were no problems encountered with my fingerprints and other tests. My two-week notice was a shock to everyone in the office I had just joined. But everyone was happy for me since everyone knew what had happened to me in the other office. Old and new colleagues told me that I did not deserve to be treated so shabbily by the agency's management and wished me the best in my new job. I was happy to leave without any guilt or hostility because I had done my job very well and had received outstanding work performance ratings during my tenure.

I started my new job on a Monday in January 1995 and to my surprise, the office had all women except for the director. I had never worked with or supervised all women in my previous jobs. It was a change, and I was happy at the time to be part of the all-woman team. Unfortunately, an all-woman environment is not necessarily the nurturing sisterhood one might imagine, and at times there could be a lot of backstabbing and general middle-school bitchiness. Cliques were not unusual and for the first few months, it was difficult for me to work in this type of environment. My years of working in a male-dominated office had left me ill prepared for dealing with employees who wanted to work individually.

After I put to good use training received in prior agencies, things began to improve; however, I shall always consider it a shame that more women do not know how to work as a team. Men, on the other hand, will normally work as a team, having learned at very young ages that working, as a team will win the game, whether it is football, basketball, or hockey. Women are great at multitasking, and if every woman learned how to work as a teammate, they would have the power to run our country smoothly and without a deficit.

Within less than a year, I was asked by the director of the office to develop, negotiate, and award a multi-million-dollar information technology contract. This contract was to serve all offices within the agency here in the United States and abroad. In addition to me, the team consisted of one attorney and ten men with engineering, information technology, and accounting backgrounds. These men were all contractors who were being paid a high salary, much more than my yearly salary. It was not easy to work with these men because they tried to override my decisions through pressure, intimidation, and their desire to defeat me at any cost. Fortunately I had worked with mostly men throughout my career and had learned to handle difficult situations.

## The Forgotten American

There was one older man by the name of Edward on our team who had a very calm demeanor, but when he became angry, he would start shouting. He would apologize quickly afterward. One day, I was on my way out of the office to go to the airport for a trip to Wright Patterson Air Force Base when he stopped me to discuss the project and team members. He wanted me to give him and a couple of other men on the team approval to make certain decisions on the project. I told him that as contractors, they were allowed to suggest and recommend but could not make decisions for federal activities that were considered to be inherently governmental functions. He went into a rage and started shouting at me, so I told him the conversation was over and left him standing there.

The next day, I received a call at my hotel from one my colleagues to tell me that Edward wanted to apologize for his ranting yesterday. I neither accepted nor declined his apology since I had enough of his bad behavior. I decided to have him removed from the project when I returned to the office the following week. Upon my return to the office, I requested the director of our office to remove Edward from the project. He wanted to know why, and I went through the number of times Edward went into rage because I would not allow certain actions to be taken by him.

The director did not want to remove him, so I went through the various federal acquisition laws and the agency policies that do not allow contractors to perform what is considered to be inherently governmental functions. I explained that an inherently governmental function is one that, as a matter of law and policy, must be performed by federal government employees and cannot be contracted out because it is intimately related to the public interest. The office director still was not willing to remove this contractor, so I asked to be removed from the project. He did not want me to be removed. After another lengthy discussion, we compromised on removing the contractor from the project and transferring him to another small project. Had I been the director, this contractor would have been terminated.

## Chapter 38

We completed the information technology project at the State Department in the early part of the summer and announced the award of the contract to the public. The next day, I received a letter from one of the vendors that competed for the contract. The International Business Management (IBM), Incorporated, protested the award to another vendor it competed against. IBM submitted its protest to the General Accountability Office (GAO), alleging that the government awarded the contract to a lesser-qualified vendor. GAO is an independent agency that serves the U.S. Congress and is often referred to as the congressional watchdog. It investigates how the federal government spends taxpayer dollars.

With the help of the team and our legal counsel, I provided several solutions for settling the protest prior to GAO making a determination on whether we followed all the laws and agency policies. The GAO would also be making a determination on whether IBM was harmed during the award process. IBM refused to discuss any alternatives and made us jump through many hurdles. One week before GAO was to provide their decision, IBM made a visit to my office and wanted to settle the protest before GAO made a decision. I told them I no longer wanted to discuss settlement issues because we had spent too much time and money on its protest. I told them I wanted GAO to make a decision.

One day before GAO was to issue its decision, I received another letter from IBM, informing me that they were withdrawing its protest. Within two hours, I received a letter by facsimile from GAO that said IBM withdrew the protest. It further stated that the case was dismissed with prejudice, meaning the case was dismissed with good reason and that IBM would be barred from bringing an action on the same claim in the future. I was so relieved since the week before, while I was having dinner with my daughter, I mentioned that I might lose a federal contract case for the first time in my career. She assured me that I would not, and she was right.

## Paula B. Compton

By early fall, our office director retired and three of us were requested to act as director on a rotating basis until he was replaced. One day in mid-summer, we were informed that only Rhonda, our colleague, would be retained as acting director. I was detailed to the Office of Federal Acquisition to help develop a multi-million-dollar contract. The other two senior staff members were to serve as section chiefs within our organization. I was comfortable with my detail since I was told I would be returning to my project at the end of the summer. In my new detail assignment, I worked with the division director and his policy analyst on a contract for drug interdiction in South America.

The pricing analyst and I worked intensely and rapidly in developing the contract so we could have a draft prior to my detail ending. When my detail ended at the end of the summer season, I returned to my former office. I was eager to continue the administration of the multimillion-dollar contract I had negotiated and awarded in the spring of that year. While I was away, Rhonda, who had been selected to serve as the acting director, was now administering the contract I had awarded.

On the day I returned to my office, I placed a call to the president of the company to which I had awarded the multi-million-dollar contract. No one answered the phone, but I did get a voicemail message that said to leave a name and a callback number. I called him several times that day but kept getting his voicemail message. I decided it would be better to set up a meeting with the president and his staff who were responsible for the contract. So I called a couple of his immediate staff members and informed them that I wanted to set up a meeting with the president and his staff for a briefing on the contract. Both staff members said they would have the president return my call and did not sound very friendly, but I figured it was a busy day for them.

Later that afternoon, I asked Rhonda to give me a briefing on what transpired on the contract while I was away. She was cordial and said she would get back to me later, but I sensed something was wrong. By noon the next day, I knew something bad was going on behind my back. Neither Rhonda nor the president of the company had gotten back to me to brief me on the status of the contract. I was in the process of sending a message to the president when the director of the Federal Acquisition Department called me—where I was detailed for the summer. She said the company president called her and requested that Rhonda continue to administer the contract. When she asked why they wanted Rhonda, the president told her the company worked much better with her. So she agreed to let Rhonda continue to administer the contract.

I was furious about the company president's request and the federal acquisition director's agreement to let Rhonda administer the contract. I told the director that I wanted the contract I developed, negotiated, and awarded returned to me as agreed when I was detailed to her office. I informed her that the contractor probably did not want me to administer the contract because they were not complying with the contract terms and conditions. I also told her that soon after I awarded the contract, the contractor's performance and delivery schedule began to deteriorate rather fast. I informed the director that one week before I was detailed to her office, I sent a letter to the contractor in which I requested better performance and staying on schedule in delivering the supplies to our embassies and consulate generals because they were still behind in their delivery schedule. I requested the contract be returned to me so I could ensure the contractor delivered the supplies so badly needed to our organizations abroad within the timeframes specified in the contract.

After a lengthy discussion, the director and I agreed to have me go back to her department to work on another multi-million-dollar contract while she sorted through the "she said, he said" situation. Later that month, an employee from the company that received the contract award called to tell me about all the "bad shenanigans" that took place while I was on detail. He informed me that the company president and Rhonda met behind closed doors at the company site several times.

Rhonda evidently had met with the president and requested the company to keep her as the manager of the contract. She had informed the president that I was too much of a "stickler" on contract law and agency rules and regulations. He evidently jumped at the chance to get rid of me so he could be free to work outside the required terms and conditions of the contract. Shortly after their meeting, the president informed his staff that Rhonda would continue to administer the contract. Evidently he told his staff that the company could now work at its own pace.

For the next month, Rhonda fought hard through her high-level management contacts to keep the contract under her jurisdiction. Her circle of high-level contacts approved all her demands. This, of course, was the straw that broke the camel's back. I could no longer sit by and let this conniving woman get away with her crooked politics. I called an acquaintance of mine on Capitol Hill (U.S. House of Representatives) and discussed my situation. He said, "Paula, when laws and rules and regulations are broken, I will always be available to help you in any way I can." With that reminder, I drafted what I considered to be a definitive and stinging memorandum to the director of federal acquisitions, my new boss, and her deputy director. In short, I said the contractor was not performing in accordance with the terms and conditions of the contract, personnel policies were being violated by Rhonda, the contract should be reassigned to another staff member if it was not going to be returned to me, and that if business continued on the same path, I would be requesting help from a friend on Capitol Hill. Within a week, the contract was assigned to another staff member, and Rhonda was ordered to work on other projects.

## Chapter 39

The following week, the director of federal acquisitions asked me if I was interested in a position abroad and that the position was currently open to federal employees only. She wanted me to apply for the position of director of the Regional Procurement Support Office (RPSO), located in the country of Singapore. This office was responsible for providing federal acquisition support to U.S. embassies and consulate generals in East Asia, the Pacific Region, and the Central and South Asia Regions. There are seventy-seven embassies and consulate generals in these locations, and they include countries from New Zealand to China to Taiwan.

I said I was interested in applying but probably did not have much chance of being selected for the position since I was very new to the organization. She encouraged me to apply anyway, so I submitted my resume that same week. It was a great shock to find out that I had been selected for the position two weeks later. I was overjoyed beyond words. By then, I had only one month and half before I had to report to the American Embassy in Singapore. I was not sure whether I could get my house leased as well as the necessary physical exams and shots completed within that timeframe. One thing was for sure: I wanted that job so badly that I set up a very ambitious schedule that some people would consider to be an impossible task.

I worked vigorously on my new project so that it would be in good standing when I left for my new assignment. I squeezed into my daily schedule the necessary physical exams and shots for living abroad. I found a real estate agent to lease my home for the next three years. In the evenings, I packed a few necessary household items to be shipped abroad to my new home.

Since I would be provided furnished housing, I decided to purchase the few appliances I would need in Singapore. This worked out very well for me after I arrived in Singapore. My beautiful young daughter, Casey, was now a full-fledged career girl. She had already served abroad and was back in the States. With her encouragement, I had applied for the overseas position. She was very happy and proud of me to get this position. While preparing to live abroad, I told her she had to save her vacation days every year so that we would travel throughout Asia, which we did for the next several years.

This was one of the most exciting times of my career. I was not only extremely happy but also very proud to be the first Navajo Indian to be selected for a director's position with a U.S Embassy abroad. I left on a Sunday morning in August to work as the director of the RPSO for the next three years. Because this is a twenty-two-hour flight, I was permitted by the agency to fly in the business class section, so it was a comfortable trip. I arrived in Singapore on Sunday evening and got my luggage, which had arrived ahead of me. I hailed a yellow cab to the hotel where I would be staying until my apartment was ready for occupancy. The hotel was a very nice one that was located close to the embassy.

On Monday morning, I went to the embassy to check in and complete all the necessary forms that had to be completed before receiving an entry badge to the Embassy. After meeting with the administrative officer and deputy chief of mission of the U.S. Embassy, I went to my office and met with my staff. Most of them could speak several languages besides English, which I found very fascinating. Upon reviewing the program that afternoon, I found that some very important and essential contracts had expired or were ready to expire. I immediately knew this was another "clean-up" job and that I would be working on weekends and long hours. I began to wonder if "sucker" was written on my forehead since I seemed to always get selected for positions that needed a "clean-up" job. I was devastated to find out that the multi-million-dollar contract for the construction of the consulate general in Ho Chi Minh was beginning to lag behind schedule. My predecessor had awarded this contract two months before my arrival in Singapore.

To add to my devastation, many U. S embassies and consulate generals in the regions were not being provided the help they needed and had been requesting for the past three years. The office in Singapore had been established to help embassies and consulate generals in the development and awarding of contracts over $100,000, but not one had been assisted to date. I received many complaints from many angry customers on not getting any type of assistance from the last director. I spent the next several months issuing instructions, guidance, explanations, and even sample documents to quiet the angry cries for help.

Once again I was in charge of cleaning up a program that was not operating at full capacity. I wondered if the director of federal acquisitions in Washington, who encouraged me to apply for the job, knew the program needed to be cleaned up. Since she was very familiar with my work history and work ethics, I started to believe she did, indeed, select me to mop up another near-disaster program. It is never healthy to lay blame on other people, and it is not within my character, so I dismissed all negative thoughts. Rolling up the proverbial sleeves, I sank

## The Forgotten American

into my work with a determination to make my office one of the best-managed organizations. From that day forward, I worked tirelessly six to seven days a week and twelve to fifteen hours a day.

## Chapter 40

Within a month of my arrival, I was able to get the construction of the new consulate general in Ho Chi Minh City, also known as Saigon during the Vietnam War, back on schedule. The construction had fallen way behind the negotiated schedule. I met twice a month with the two American engineers, supervising the construction to make sure it stayed on schedule and that all contract requirements were met. I always flew to Ho Chi Minh on Singapore Airlines, which I consider to be one of the best airlines on which I have traveled. I always received excellent service.

The contractor who was selected to build the consulate general had an office in New York City and Ho Chi Min City. The contractor quite often became uncooperative, demanding additional payments for work that he considered to be outside the scope of the contract. We had many unpleasant meetings through conference calls with the contractor. Time after time, the engineers and I were forced to remind the contractor the contents of the engineering blueprints, not to mention the terms and conditions of the contract they signed in good faith. I was responsible for making sure the contractor complied with the terms and conditions of the contract and that they were paid in a timely manner. The engineers were responsible for ensuring the building was constructed in accordance with the engineering blueprints.

My visits to the construction site usually included briefings from the two engineers, in addition to resolving or making decisions on issues as they arose. On every visit, I would put on my hardhat and tour the construction site. I met many of the Vietnamese construction workers, but unfortunately none of them spoke English, so I could not exchange pleasantries with them. However, the leader of the two-member engineering team spoke Vietnamese fluently. We were very fortunate to get an American engineer who spoke fluent Vietnamese. I admired his ability to give direction and guidance to the Vietnamese construction workers. His knowledge of the Vietnamese language contributed to the successful completion of the building.

Six months into the construction of the new building, the engineering office within the Department of State wanted to know when we expected to have the consulate general building completed. We informed its staff that we expected the building to be completed within one year from the date the construction started. They laughed at us and said there was no way it could be completed in one year. Working as a team, we proved them wrong. The building was, indeed, completed in one year with no defects and no additional costs to the contract.

I often stayed in Ho Chi Minh City at my own expense to do some touring in the hinterlands. The hotel concierge, who made sure I had an English-speaking driver and guide, normally arranged my tours. I once had a professor from the university there in Ho Chi Minh City as a guide. I toured everything from old historic sites to old war museums. I even crawled for a quarter of a mile in one of the Vietnam War underground tunnels. Some of these tunnels had small kitchenettes and sleeping rooms.

Many parts of Vietnam were still virgin territory when I went on these tours in Ho Chi Minh. The hinterlands that I was able to tour were beautiful with clear skies and fresh air. After I returned to the U.S., one of my Vietnamese acquaintances said that sometime after 2002, Vietnam had changed considerably. Around this time, Vietnam opened its doors to outside merchants from countries such as the United States and Europe.

My daughter, Casey, and I toured Vietnam at Christmas time in 2000. I was so happy to spend time with her. We had a wonderful time sightseeing, shopping, and eating all kinds of Vietnamese dishes on our whirlwind tour. On the first day of our tour, we flew to Hanoi, the capital of Vietnam and the second-largest city. From Hanoi we traveled by car to Halong Bay, located on the coast of northern Vietnam. There we took an all-day boat cruise and saw some of the 1,926 beautiful islands located on the bay. Lunch served with Vietnamese wine was absolutely scrumptious. We returned to Hanoi and spent a day touring the city and the famous Army museum. From Hanoi we flew down to Hue (pronounced "Hway"), which is famous for its Imperial City. We toured palaces, castles, royal temples, gardens, and artificial canals within the Imperial City. After a day of touring in Hue, we traveled by car to Da Nang City, a dominant port and the fourth-largest city in Vietnam. One of the most interesting sites in Da Nang City was the war museum, located on the grounds of the Ho Chi Minh museum. It has all kinds of rusty remnants of the Vietnam War.

After spending one and half days in Da Nang City, we took a flight down to Ho Chi Minh City. It is the largest city, the economic capital, and the cultural trendsetter of Vietnam. It is the heart and soul of Vietnam. We spent a couple of days there touring, shopping and eating wonderful Vietnamese food before returning home to Singapore. We had great English-speaking drivers and guides on this whirlwind tour. They were very gracious and great storytellers.

My job as director of the RPSO required me to travel to many American embassies and consulate generals in many different countries. Sometimes my trips were back to back, and I would be exhausted upon returning home to Singapore. While in these countries, I usually stayed through Saturday to do some touring, which was always at my own expense. Many of the local people in these countries thought I was one of the local people, which I found to be complimentary and puzzling at the same time.

For example, while in New Zealand, people in that country thought I was a Morai; in Australia, they thought I was part Australian Aborigine; in China, I was believed to be Chinese; in Korea, I was considered Korean; in the Philippines, I was thought to be Filipino; in Malaysia, I was believed to be Malaysian; and so forth. When they did find out I am a Native American, they displayed their sympathy. It was surprising to find out that many knew the tragic history of the Native Americans, which many referred to as genocide. Many wanted to know why the Native Americans stayed in America and if they still had allegiance to America. My definitive response was always: "We hold full and complete allegiance to America despite our tragic history; we love America and will never leave it or turn against it."

## Chapter 41

In my business travels abroad to various embassies and consulate generals, airports varied in services. Some airports had excellent check-in airline services, and some had poor and inefficient check-in services. Some airports had separate lines for people with diplomatic passports to enter the flight departure area. As a diplomat, I used these lines, which very often only had a few people in line to be checked into the departure area. I no longer have access to using those lines while traveling abroad. I truly miss those wonderful privileges, especially in today's travel environment, where people have to stand in line for hours.

One trip I made to Shenyang, China, will forever be ingrained in my brain. In early August in 2000, the "Consul General," hereafter referred to as "Consul," for the Shenyang "Consulate General", called me. He said the construction office in Washington, D.C., asked him to get help from my office. He explained that he notified them of the damages done to the Consulate in March during the riots held around the complex. College students, with the help of some local communities, held anti-American demonstrations that turned into riots resulting in severe damages. The Consul had repeatedly informed the Washington office that the repairs needed to be done before September due to the fall weather being very cold in that part of the country. He had warned them that he expected an early winter that year.

I guess the Washington construction office kept putting off the work until August, when he sent an emergency request to get the work done. They notified him within minutes that same day, informing him that they were short of people and could not help him. They recommended that he contact the director of the RPSO in Singapore to get help. When he called me, he sounded stressed out and very unhappy. He told me the full story of the damages and actions he had taken to try to find a contractor in China to do the repair work. He found only one that could do the work. I told him we needed to get special approval from Washington to use one contractor. I further informed him that we needed to take some shortcuts, which would omit certain mandatory contracting procedures, but in order to do so; we also needed special approval from Washington. I gave him instructions on whom to contact in writing for the special approval and assured him I would also follow up with the same request for approval from my management. Fortunately, we both were able to get the special approval in one week.

After getting the necessary approvals to proceed with the construction repair work, I developed a draft contract and other required documents. Time was of the essence since we were now in week three of August 2000. The Consul and I went over the draft contract by telephone and made the necessary changes. After refining the draft contract, I set up the negotiation session for the last week in August. I anticipated completing negotiations and signing the contract with the Chinese contractor from Beijing, China, that week.

A bother and sister both trained engineers owned the Chinese company. They attended a university in Germany, where they learned to speak both German and English. The sister remained in Germany for a number of years working for a construction company and had returned to Beijing the previous two years to manage the company for her brother. I did a search on the company and found the company to be "best of the best" in China, so I was confident we would indeed have a contract signed in one week. Based on my search, I also anticipated getting excellent repair work to be completed within a month.

To save on my travel budget, it was normal practice for me to do site visits to at least two or three embassies or consulate generals. In preparing for my trip to Shenyang, China, I had my administrative assistant book a flight to Beijing first and then to Shenyang. Since my business in Beijing would take only two days, I left Singapore on a Wednesday morning. During my two-day visit to the American Embassy in Beijing, I attended many meetings and provided guidance on various contract projects. I was not scheduled to leave for Shenyang until Sunday, so I booked a guided tour for Saturday. My tour included Tiananmen Square, the heart of the 1989 Pro-Democracy demonstration and situated in the heart of Beijing; the Forbidden City, built between A.D. 1406 and 1420; and the Summer Palace, which was once the summer residence of the Qing Dynasty emperors. My tour was not only educational but also relaxing and enjoyable.

The next morning, I checked out of the hotel and headed for the airport. The cab driver wanted to know if I wished to be let off on the international departure side or the local flight side. I told him the local side, where he let me off to fight the crowd. When I flew to Beijing earlier in the week, I arrived on the international departure side of the airport. That section of the airport was clean, with many good restaurants and shops.

After fighting a mass of people, I finally made my way to the local check-in section. Just about everybody spoke only Chinese in this section. Several of us tried to form one line to the check-in counter, but we were not successful. Finally

## The Forgotten American

one tall Chinese man spoke very loudly, and everyone fell into line. Since he was a very tall and mean-looking man, everyone obeyed except for one skinny lady. I was the first one in line, but that did not matter to her; she went past me and up to the counter. Some people grumbled and the huge man said something to her, but she paid no attention. Later, I found out from the Consul in Shenyang that this type of behavior is common practice by many in China. He said that happened all the time at the grocery stores in Shenyang, and it drove his wife crazy.

It was amazing how things changed from one section of the airport to another in Beijing. The bathrooms in the local section were very untidy, and there were very few restaurants or shops in this part of the airport. To add to the unpleasant atmosphere, the plane was delayed by one hour and thirty minutes. When the plane finally arrived for boarding, I quickly got in what I thought would be an orderly line, but to my surprise, no single line was formed. Everyone just crowded on top of one another to get on the plane. The small plane used for local travel did not look too sturdy, and to make matters worse, people were loaded down with all kinds of bags and boxes as they entered the plane. I thought for sure some of the people were going to start loading live chickens on the plane. But no live animals accompanied the travelers, and all the bags and boxes were able to be stored in the storage bins.

After a rough seventy-minute flight, I arrived in Shenyang around 9:00 P.M. The cab driver did not speak English but did recognize the name of the hotel I stated to him. Upon arrival at the hotel, I was warmly greeted by one of the hotel clerks. This was a very large hotel used by many U.S. firms such as ITT, John Deere, Boeing, Dell, and other major U.S. firms that have made significant investments in the region. Therefore, most of the employees at the check-in desk spoke English.

The rooms were very clean, spacious, and had room service until midnight. Since I had not eaten since breakfast, I ordered a large bowl of wonton soup, which was delivered within a few minutes by a very hospitable young man. I eat just about anything as long as it is piping hot from the stove, microwave, or open pit for cooking. I have eaten many different types of food while traveling abroad and have never gotten ill from them.

The next morning, I stopped at the front desk to get a map of the city and to find out how far the Consulate was from the hotel where I was staying. The hotel receptionist gave me some courtesy cards written in both Chinese and English to give to the cab drivers as I traveled around the city. All I had to do was write in the name of the place to which I was going and give it to the cab driver. The card gave brief instructions on my destinations in Chinese and English. The hotel receptionist explained that all the cab drivers did not speak English, and it was necessary for me to have these cards available at all times while in Shenyang.

I arrived at the Consulate at 7:45 A.M., which was not far from my hotel, but unfortunately it was not within walking distance. I was shocked to see so many windows boarded up. The Consulate was within a compound consisting of housing for employees. It was protected by cement wall approximately eight feet tall. I was further shocked to find the compound to be only inches away from the main city road. All new embassies and consulate generals today are required to have a certain amount of space between the building and the public roads. It was obvious that the building needed a lot of repairs done before the start of the winter season.

The guards who were stationed outside the compound wall met me. After providing the necessary identifications, I was escorted into the building, where the administrative assistant met me. The Consul is responsible for managing the affairs of the Consulate. It has a major role in the management of the close relationship the United States has with northeast China.

I was introduced to the Consul, a tall, slender, and friendly man. I wanted to get the full story on the destruction of the building, so for the next thirty minutes he briefed me on what happened in the spring of fiscal year 2000. He said the compound was nearly destroyed by local protestors and rioters who were mainly students from local universities. He said it was strange to see even the local police encouraging the people to pick up rocks and throw them at the compound. The police were supposed to protect the compound, but instead they appeared to side with the protestors.

I asked the Consul whether the employees living in the compound were frightened. He said all of the employees appeared to be calm until late in the afternoon, when most of the windows that could be seen above the compound walls were broken. He said that around 9:00 P.M., the rioters had all departed the area and the streets were empty and quiet. Since he was concerned for the safety of his employees, he took them in a van to one of the hotels that normally accommodate Americans and other foreign visitors. Only a few employees live and work in the compound, so they were all able to fit in the van. As the Consul, he had to return to the building to monitor the compound and to communicate with his management in Washington, D.C. Fortunately for him, the protestors never returned that night or the next day. He said the day after the riot; it was unusual and rather funny to find the local Chinese people on the streets very hospitable and friendly. He said they acted like nothing bad had ever happened.

After meeting with the Consul, I was led to a conference room, where I was to hold negotiations with the contractor we had selected to repair the damages to the building. Upon the arrival of the contractor from Beijing, China, he was introduced to me, and we exchanged greetings as well as business cards. I had requested that the Consul attend the negotiation session, which I expected to last all week. Before arriving in Shenyang, I had informed him that it would be necessary to review the contract with the contractor. This meant going over every paragraph of the contract to make sure the contractor understood the type of supplies and services he was to provide in the construction repair job. The Consul requested that I negotiate a completion date of one month, if at all possible, because he did not want his employees to freeze to death. I told him I would do my best.

The negotiation session started out very well that Monday morning because the young Chinese contractor spoke good English. We moved at a pretty good pace in reviewing the contract document. Each time I asked the contractor if he understood and agreed to the terms and conditions, he would say, "I suppose." Finally, I decided I better stop the session and make sure the phrase "I suppose," meant, "yes." So I called for a coffee break, at which time I met privately with the Consul and asked him if the contractor meant, "Yes, I agree," when he said, "I suppose." He confirmed that indeed it meant, "Yes, I agree."

The negotiation session went very well the next several days, and we were able to finish our negotiation session by 4:00 P.M. on the third day. I spent the next day making the necessary changes to the contract, which I was able to complete and submit to the Consul for review by the close of business. On Friday morning, I met with him to see if he had any issues with the final version of the contract. There were none, so as the authorized representative of the federal government, I signed the contract. We called the contractor to let him know the contract had been signed and Federal Express-China was sending a copy to him. Since this construction repair work was urgent and compelling, the Consul requested that the work begin that following Monday. I was able to negotiate a completion date of one month for the repair of the Consulate.

I completed my business by 10:00 A.M. that Friday and my flight back to Singapore was not until 2:30 P.M., so I decided to visit the Shenyang Imperial Palace. The palace is located in Shenyang's Old City, about eight miles from the Consulate. Shenyang Imperial Palace Museum is the most ancient imperial architectural complex of the Chinese Qing dynasty. It is next only to the Forbidden City in Beijing in historical and artistic value.

I very much enjoyed the ancient imperial architecture and its abundant collections of imperial relics, such as the sword once used by the Nurhachi, the Manchu chieftain who was the first king of the Jin State that was established in 1616. Unfortunately, no one is allowed to take pictures, but it was indeed an enjoyable tour for me. I stopped my tour around 12:00 P.M. and hailed a taxi to get back to my hotel to check out and to go to the airport.

My flight back to Singapore was scheduled to take nine hours, but I was glad it was a direct flight since I was very much exhausted by this time. The journey back to Singapore on China Southern Airlines, the world's sixth-largest airline measured by passengers carried, was very comfortable.

## Chapter 42

Another trip that will be forever ingrained in my brain is my trip to Colombo, Sri Lanka. The island country of Sri Lanka is in the emerald green waters of the Indian Ocean off the southern coast of India. Colombo is the largest city and commercial capital of Sri Lanka and is located on the west coast of the island. The island's population consisted of the Sinhalese majority and Tamil separatists. It was long known as Ceylon but changed its name to Sri Lanka in 1972. Tensions between the Sinhalese majority and Tamil separatists erupted into a civil war in 1983, and tens of thousands died in that ethnic conflict. Although there are no more civil wars, social and governmental conflicts still exist today between the Sinhalese majority and Tamil separatists.

At the request of the U.S. Embassy in Colombo, Sri Lanka, I had scheduled a trip in the month of July to provide assistance to them. But due to the travel red alert from the U.S. Department of State, I had to cancel my trip three times. Travel alerts are issued to provide information about short-term conditions within particular countries that pose risks to the security of U.S. citizens. The travel alert for Sri Lanka was to caution U.S. citizens about terrorist attacks in the country. While the alerts were ongoing, the embassy was getting impatient because it needed immediate assistance. In its last urgent call to get assistance, its staff informed me that it was safe to travel in the city of Colombo and that it was very safe in the surrounding areas of the embassy.

It was not safe to travel to Sri Lanka because the rebels called Tamil Tigers were launching a campaign of violence and bloodshed throughout the country. The Tamil Tigers are among the most dangerous and deadly extremists in the world. They have launched a campaign of violence for more than three decades. Their goal is to seize control of the country from the Sinhalese ethnic majority and create an independent Tamil state. Through the years, they have launched suicide attacks, assassinated politicians, taken hostages, and committed other crimes to finance their operation.

I finally got tired of waiting for the red alert to go away, so I called the embassy and told them I would be there to help them the second week in September. A week before my departure to Colombo, some of my colleagues kept telling me that I would be dodging bullets in Sri Lanka. I ignored all the negative comments and kept my travel schedule in place. The embassy staff in Colombo had waited patiently long enough, and their cry for help was becoming more urgent every day. Based on my life experience, when it comes to turmoil anywhere in the world, it usually is not as bad as it is reported. Thus, I did not worry too much about my trip.

A week before my departure to Sri Lanka, I got an urgent message from my management in Washington, D.C. They wanted me to meet them in Frankfurt, Germany, for a conference the same week I was scheduled to provide assistance to the Colombo Embassy people. I told them I could not go since I had a trip to Sri Lanka that was urgent and which I had delayed for a month due to the turmoil in that country. They turned a deaf ear and requested I cancel my trip, and when I told them I could not cancel the trip, they insisted I shorten my trip. They further suggested that, if necessary, I could travel all night to Frankfurt so I could be at the conference on Thursday morning. I was shocked and angry to be treated in such a manner.

As requested, I did shorten my trip to Colombo by leaving on a Sunday so I could start my business early Monday morning rather than on a Tuesday. Prior to leaving, I had made arrangements with the Colombo Embassy officials to work with them on Monday and Tuesday, and if necessary I would make a second trip the following month. They were satisfied with the plan, so I left for Sir Lanka on Sunday morning so that I could arrive there before noon. I wanted to take a quick tour of the City that afternoon if I found the city to be safe for touring.

When I arrived in Colombo, everything seemed to be peaceful until I exited the airport to get to my hotel. Men from the Sri Lankan Armed Forces and Sri Lanka Corps of Military Police were present everywhere. They evidently were there to monitor the flow of human traffic and to guard the various entrances to the airport. The scene was a little scary, but I figured I was safe under their watch. Before I could get a cab, one military man stopped me and wanted to see my passport.

The military police looked at my passport and handed it back to me. With broken English and a very heavy accent, he asked me where I was going and if I had business in Sri Lanka. It was hard to understand him, but I got the gist of the questions. Before I could respond, another military man approached, and he spoke in his own language, which I did not understand. They motioned me to come back with them into the airport. At this point, I began to get somewhat frightened, but I did my best to remain calm. I don't think my body language indicated that I was frightened. I knew it would do no good to stand there and try to explain why I was

## The Forgotten American

traveling in the country of Sri Lanka, so I followed them into the airport without saying anything. While following the men, I wondered if anyone would find me if anything drastic happened.

I was led to a small room, where two military men who wanted to see my passport again met me. One was an interpreter who spoke English with a very heavy accent, so it was hard to understand him. He started asking me questions that were presented to him by the man who did not speak English. I explained why I was in Sri Lanka and that my work with the American Embassy in Colombo would be for only two days. About ten minutes into the questioning session, I was asked if I was Asian. I informed the two men that I was Native American— or American Indian, as we were once called. I said I worked for the American Embassy in the county of Singapore and that my job as director was to provide assistance in the area of federal contracting to various embassies in the East Asia and Pacific Region and the Central and South Asia Region.

The man who did not speak English jumped up and shook my hand. The interpreter said he was very pleased to meet the first American Indian and that what white America did to them was very atrocious. He went on to say that white America likes to say there was no genocide against the American Indians but everyone in the world knows they tried to eradicate them. He went on to say that white America likes to accuse other countries of genocide while it hides the atrocities it did to the Native Americans. He asked me the one question that is always asked of me: "Do Native Americans like America, and why did they not leave it?" I responded like I did so many times throughout my travels: "We hold full and complete allegiance to America despite our tragic history; we love America and will never leave it or turn against it."

With that, the questioning ended and the two men escorted me back outside to catch a cab. On the way out, I asked whether the Tamil Tigers were causing turmoil in Colombo. He said all the fighting was in the hinterlands of Sri Lanka and that the city of Colombo was safe from all terrorist activities. As we walked out the front entrance, the man who did not speak English said something to the rest of the military men posted outside. It must have been good, because they all looked at me and nodded with approval. I quickly jumped into the first cab that drove up to the curb and directed the driver to my hotel.

On the way to the hotel, I realized my knees had gone weak and my mouth had become dry from the frightening situation I had just experienced. I felt as though I had dodged a bullet, as the saying goes, and on the way to the hotel wondered what might have happened had I been a Caucasian woman or man. Would the person have been detained and questioned or simply ignored? Since most of the American people in the embassy were of the Caucasian race, I assumed the military men would not have detained anyone of that race. It was good to know the Sri Lankans knew the history of the Native Americans. I am sad, however, to point out that today many Americans do not know anything or know very little about Native Americans. No wonder many Europeans refer to Native Americans as the "Forgotten Americans." I believe we are truly the "Forgotten Americans."

On Monday morning, I decided to walk from my hotel to the American Embassy since I was in safe territory, which was only three blocks from my hotel. The embassy officials and I worked long hours for the next two days. We were able to complete all the tasks that needed attention and fixing within those two days. I did not have to return to Colombo the following month, and everyone was satisfied with the work we completed. I felt good about our accomplishments and for some strange reason felt rejuvenated for my next round of flights the next day to Frankfurt, Germany.

## Chapter 43

The next morning, I caught a flight to Frankfurt, Germany, as I had been directed to do so by my management in Washington, D.C. My administrative assistant had booked a flight on Kuwait Airways from Colombo, Si Lanka, to Kuwait International Airport, where I was to change to a bigger plane for Frankfurt. Considering what a wealthy country Kuwait is, I was very disappointed in the design and appearance of the plane. Kuwait Airways is the national airline of Kuwait, based in Kuwait City and wholly owned by the Kuwaiti government.

Later that week, I mentioned to my daughter that Kuwait Airways was a disappointment and that such a wealthy country should have big fancy airplanes. She reminded me of the destruction of many infrastructures caused by the 1990 invasion. She also said many Kuwaitis don't travel on commercial airlines since they can afford to fly their private jet planes to anywhere they wish to travel.

Because of the changes in time zones, my administrative assistant had selected a flight that was to get me to Frankfurt by noon so that I could get some rest. I told her I didn't require much sleep, but she insisted I needed to rest at least half a day in Frankfurt for the next day's heavy schedule.

As we took off on Kuwait Airways, it sounded like it was ready to break. The seats were structured poorly and had hardly any legroom, and the food served left much to be desired. Kuwait Airways was a far cry from Singapore Airlines, which I normally used for my business trips. Upon arrival in Kuwait, I quickly went to the Lufthansa Airlines departure section and checked in for my seat assignment. While I was checking in, the woman processing my ticket said my plane was delayed by two hours. After checking in, I started walking around the airport, which left a lot to be desired. It did not have the appearance of an international airport. To my disappointment, there were only a few shops and restaurants, and the waiting lounges were poorly furnished.

I was to depart on Lufthansa Airlines from Kuwait City at 1:00 P.M. and arrive in Frankfurt by 4:20 P.M., a five-hour-forty-five-minute flight. There is a one-hour time change from Kuwait City to Frankfurt, Germany—one hour behind Kuwait time. Due to the two-hour delay, I figured I would not arrive in Frankfurt until 9:00 P.M.

With all the time changes from Singapore to Sri Lanka to Kuwait to Frankfurt, I was not quite sure if I was tired or not. I never believed in resting during the day since to me it is a waste of time. As my grandmother used to say to me and the rest of her grandchildren: "If you sleep late or during the day, you will be poor the rest of your life." To this day, none of us sleep late or during the day even though we no longer believe in such tales.

Our flight on Lufthansa Airlines finally left around 4:00 P.M., making my arrival even later than 9:00 P.M. On this flight, there were many Kuwaitis and Arabs dressed in Muslim attire. I wanted to sleep during the flight but could not, so I just prepared for my conference presentation for the next day. Upon arrival, I stopped at the restroom to freshen up before going to the baggage terminal. To my surprise, there was a check-in area just before the main customs check-in location. One security guard handled this single pre-custom check-in point with two men on each side of him with guns strapped to their hips.

I figured that with the pre-check-in line moving so slowly, I would not be able to get to my hotel until around 11:00 P.M. I stepped out of line a couple of times to see why it was moving so slowly. The man checking the passports appeared to be reviewing each passport presented to him by a Muslim, Kuwaiti, or Arab. I found this to be offensive and discriminatory but told myself there must be a reason for such scrutiny. I was digging in my briefcase when one of the German security guards walked up to me and asked to see my passport. After looking at me briefly, he escorted me to the front and told me to continue to the customs area. I did not ask any questions but moved as quickly as I could.

Having a diplomatic passport helped me get to the customs area without a lot of scrutiny. However, when I got to the customs desk, the man looked at my passport and then at me several times before he asked where I was going. Upon telling him I had business at the American Consulate General, he asked what kind of business I was on. I came very close to telling him it was none of his business but said ever so politely that it was American Embassy business that could not be revealed without the approval of the embassy. He gave a smirk and let me go through the security gate.

Upon my arrival at the hotel, I received a message from my daughter, Casey. She had left me the name of the flight she was taking from the Washington Dulles Airport and the time of her arrival in Frankfurt that Friday evening. Two weeks before leaving for my two-week business trip, I told her that my last stop was Frankfurt, Germany. Since flights to Frankfurt were inexpensive at that time of the year, she wanted to join me for the weekend. This was good because the conference I was to attend ended that Friday evening. So we had arranged to meet

## The Forgotten American

at my hotel on Friday evening and take the all-day Rhine River tour on Saturday.

The next day, we caught the Rhine River Cruise, traveling first by bus on the Autobahn Road; however, we did not see too many speeding cars. In reality, the Autobahn looks like a typical freeway and everyone is not driving at the speed of sound. I found out on this trip that many sections of the Autobahn do, in fact, have speed limits, and such was the case with the road we traveled on.

We took the Middle Rhine River day tour, which was indeed relaxing and fun. Casey and I truly enjoyed visiting, as well as tasting wine at the various locations we stopped. The Middle Rhine is also popularly known as the Romantic Rhine Valley because of the scenic views and the many beautiful castles and ruins along the riverbanks. Unusually, the wine tasting took place in caves along the Rhine; however, this curiosity aside, the microclimate of the Middle Rhine area produces some of the best wine and fruit. It was wonderful, indeed! Our one-day tour was just too short, but we both had fun and the time we spent together was worth a million dollars.

We were both scheduled to fly to our respective homes on Sunday morning, Casey back to the U.S. and me to Singapore. That morning Casey and I went to the airport together at 4:00 A.M. since both of our flights were scheduled to depart around the same time. I had a nonstop flight, and Casey had a one-stop flight through Copenhagen. Her departure flight on Lufthansa was at 7:15 A.M., and mine was at 6:38 A.M. on Singapore Airlines. I was very sad to see her leave, but I was also happy that I got to see her over the weekend even though it was a very short visit. I was glad I was flying home on Singapore Airlines since the flight duration was twelve hours and fifteen minutes. At least it was going to be a comfortable ride home with good food and cheerful and polite flight attendants. My trip back to Singapore was indeed relaxing.

## Chapter 44

I had been studying and analyzing the requests for assistance from the various American embassies and consulate generals in the East Asia and Pacific Region and the Central and South Asia Region for one whole year. Based on my analysis, I made a decision to close the Singapore RPSO. During the one-year analysis period, I found many acquisition offices within the various embassies and consulate generals requesting assistance with acquisitions under the $100,000 threshold. When the RPSO was established, it was intended to provide assistance to embassies and consulate generals for the acquisition of supplies and services that had a value of $100,000 and above. Not too many embassies and consulate generals have a need to acquire supplies or services that exceed that threshold.

Based on my findings, I sent a decision memorandum to my management in Washington, D.C. I recommended closing the Singapore RPSO and relocating that responsibility to a larger U.S. Embassy. Copies of this decision memorandum were also issued to senior officials who were responsible for the embassies and consulate generals in the two regions. Many of these embassies and consulates had gotten in the habit of asking for assistance from the Singapore office with acquisitions under $100,000. Prior to sending my decision memorandum, I was constantly reminding them of the original intent for the establishment of the RPSO in Singapore, which too often fell on deaf ears.

My decision memorandum provided the reasons in detail for closing the RPSO in Singapore. It also recommended that the support office be relocated to a much bigger U.S. embassy like the Embassy in Bangkok, Thailand, or the U.S. Embassy in Manila, Philippines. The larger embassies had many more staff members in their acquisition offices and had larger budgets to provide the necessary acquisition support to various embassies and consulate generals in these two regions.

It took about two months before the Washington, D.C. office, made a decision. I was pleased to hear that my recommendation was accepted and that my management in Washington would start searching for a new location where the new support office would be relocated for the two regions. It took another six months before a decision was made to relocate the responsibilities to the U.S. consulate general in Frankfurt, Germany. The Frankfurt Regional Support Office certainly could handle the extra workload. It had a very large staff to handle the acquisition of supplies and services for embassies and consulate generals located in the Europe and Eurasia Regions. It was determined that they were also capable of providing support to the two regions in Asia.

I had arranged to have the Singapore RPSO closed when my assignment at the U.S. Embassy ended. I still had more clean-up work to do for the Singapore acquisition office. I also wanted to provide additional training to my staff, award new contracts, and modify existing contracts to keep the embassy operating efficiently. In addition, some embassies still needed my assistance with their acquisitions that were over the threshold of $100,000. After the decision to close our office as the regional support office, our workload, especially mine, decreased to a reasonable level so that we could now complete the "clean-up" job in our office.

With the workload coming down to a decent level, I was now able to go to my Tai Chi classes on a regular basis and to my reflexology and body massage sessions on Sundays. I discovered that the Tai Chi exercises and reflexology sessions were methods used by the Chinese people for health and longevity. Despite the long hours at the office, I was now able to have at least one full day of healthy, relaxing activities.

## Chapter 45

One assignment at the embassy that I did not enjoy was serving as duty officer for one week every other month. Our services were provided in the evenings during the workweek and twenty-four hours on weekends. All embassy employees at the senior management level were required to serve as duty officers for the U.S. Embassy. For me this duty was in addition to my ten to fifteen work hours a day, six to seven days a week.

As embassy duty officers, we were to provide assistance to American citizens living or visiting in the country of Singapore. The assistance we provided ranged from offering information on medical facilities, obtaining emergency funds from the U.S. for individuals or families, and helping U.S. citizens in distress, including being destitute, arrested, severely sick, or separated from their family. During the regular workweek and normal business hours, the embassy consular office was responsible for providing these types of assistance.

For some strange reason, when my turn came around to serve as duty officer, there was always an emergency of some kind that kept me working into the early-morning hours. One evening, I received a call from the embassy guards, requesting that I call a certain hotel to help the manager with a deceased American. I normally did not drive my car during these times since it was faster and less expensive to catch a cab. In addition, every cab driver knew the nooks and crannies of the city and could get you to your destination within minutes. The cab driver got me to the hotel within ten minutes, and I immediately went to work identifying the man.

The hotel manager told me that he had called the medical examiner to verify that the man was, indeed, deceased. He took me to the room, and I was introduced to the medical examiner. I asked if the American was deceased and, if so, for how long. He said that based on his exam, the man had been dead from what appeared to be a heart attack for more than eight hours. After a brief discussion on the deceased man, the medical examiner and his assistant left the manger and me to continue our work.

The hotel manager and I looked around for his passport and fortunately for us, it was in the hotel safe, which was open. His briefcase had his travel papers, which identified the company for whom he worked. After making sure the man in the bed was the man in the passport photo, I told the manager I would notify his company. His travel papers indicated that he was on a business trip for a company located in New York City. The hotel manager insisted that he give me an office where I could take care of the necessary paperwork and notifications. He led me to a big fancy office, where I went to work.

After several back-and-forth communications with the company for whom the deceased man worked, we agreed it would be best if the company notified his family. The company requested to take over from there so they could make arrangements to fly their employee's body home. They said they would work with the hotel manager on getting the body to the airport and would contact me if necessary. I requested the company contact me when they got the body on board for the flight back to New York City. I went home and wrote up my report, and by that time, it was 1:40 A.M.

Another time while serving as the embassy duty officer, the embassy's Marine Guards notified me at 10:30 P.M. of a request that I call the customs office at Singapore Changi Airport. They said a Navy man, who was en route from New York, lost his passport and needed to get permission to enter the country of Singapore. I called the airport customs office and informed the man in charge that I was the American embassy duty officer who would be meeting the young Navy man at its customs office. I asked for a description of the Navy man. I was told that he was an American citizen of Mexican descent who was dressed in non-military attire. They said the plane was expected to arrive at midnight. So, like my normal practice, I called a cab to go to the airport. It was 11:15 P.M. by the time I left for the airport.

On the way to the airport, as some people do, I stereotyped the Navy man. I am ashamed to admit it, but I visualized him as having dark skin and being short in stature. I visualized him that way because I grew up in the state of New Mexico, where many young Mexicans were dark skinned and short in stature. Although many of us today don't want or like to stereotype people, we do so because of our environment during our formative years. I do not believe this fits in the category of being a racist, but some may call it that these days.

When I arrived at the customs office, I saw this tall, handsome young man with a great physique that looked more like an Italian. The young Chinese and Malaysian girls were all giggling and staring at him. Enjoying all the attention, he paced back and forth. He knew he was a very handsome man and probably would have liked staying near the girls for another hour, but I interrupted him. I introduced myself as the U.S. Embassy Duty Officer and was there to give him permission to enter the country of Singapore. I informed him that the U.S. Marine

## The Forgotten American

Embassy Guards had notified me concerning his lost billfold containing both his driver's license and passport. He confirmed that it was true.

He said he boarded his flight from the JFK International Airport in New York City and changed planes in San Francisco, where he was not required to check in again. He said he carried his airline tickets in his shirt pocket and had barely enough time to go from the United Airlines section to the international departure area to catch his flight to Singapore. It was not until they were flying over the Pacific Ocean he realized his billfold and his passport were missing. He said his driver's license was in his billfold, along with his travel money. Evidently, he immediately notified the flight attendants to call ahead to the customs office at the Singapore Changi Airport. The message from the Singapore Airport was delivered to the U.S. Embassy, and the embassy staff notified me as soon as they got the message.

The U.S. Marine Embassy Guards had informed me that the young Navy man only had his Navy dog tag and his transfer papers to the U.S. Navy base on the island of Diego Garcia, located in the heart of the Indian Ocean. So I requested to see his dog tag and transfer papers. I checked his dog tag, which looked legitimate, and his transfer papers were original copies and appeared to be authentic. I wanted to be absolutely sure that he was being transferred by the Navy, so I called the defense attaché who had an office at the U.S. Embassy and who was listed as being on call that night. After waking her up and briefing her on the subject matter, she said he was, indeed, on his way to Diego Garcia. She said he and another woman who was a chaplain were to board a military plane that morning around 10:00 A.M.

After confirming his identification, we proceeded to the airport customs office. On the way, he turned to me and said I had a very interesting job, and he would like to have one like that. I chuckled and said to him, "This is one of other duties, as assigned by the U.S. Embassy." I told him I was one of the directors at the embassy and worked anywhere from ten to fifteen hours a day, six to seven days a week. He was very surprised and said, "So you have not gone to bed yet since yesterday morning?" I said yes and that I was one of the few fortunate people in the world who did not require much sleep.

After providing my diplomatic passport and identification as an embassy duty officer to the customs office, I authorized the young Navy man to enter the country of Singapore. We made our way back to the main part of the airport, where the chaplain was waiting for us. She was a young Caucasian female, quiet but friendly. I asked if they knew where they were to depart that morning, but they were not too sure. I made some more calls to find the exact location where they were to board the military aircraft that was to take them to the U.S. Navy base.

Without his wallet, the young man had no money and therefore had no means with which to purchase refreshments. He and the chaplain looked tired, and I felt very bad for them since I know how tiring it is to fly for twenty-two hours. I found it necessary to give the chaplain fifty dollars of my own money. I told them the airport rest area had private showers for ten dollars per person should they desire to take one. I figured that after their showers, they would have enough money for breakfast. It was now 3:45 A.M., so I gave them my cell, home, and office number in case they ran into problems. I wished them a safe trip and headed home.

Another incident while serving as the embassy duty officer was a very unpleasant incident that made me want to punish the young man myself. One evening while preparing to leave my office around 7:00 P.M., the Marine Embassy Guard came to my office and said; "I knew I could find you here." I knew right there and then that something horrible had happened and I would have to take care of it. The Marine Guard gave me the scoop on a young Vietnamese man who was arrested.

This young man, in his early twenties, was a U.S. citizen traveling on business for an information technology company out of the Washington Metropolitan area. Evidently, he and his colleagues arrived in Singapore on Saturday morning and decided to go to the country of Malaysia on Sunday. While touring Malaysia, a neighboring country of Singapore, this young man bought compact discs with pornographic material. He put them in a shopping bag thinking he could get them through the Singapore border customs area without any problem. What he did not know is that Singapore customs officers have and use the best high-technology equipment. While living there, I often told my colleagues that I suspected they had hidden cameras everywhere, even at the park where I ran every other day.

When returning to Singapore, to the surprise of the young U.S. Vietnamese man, the Singapore border customs authorities asked him to put his shopping bag through the x-ray machine. The machine revealed the pornographic material, and the authorities arrested him there at the border. Singapore customs authorities enforce strict regulations for the import and export of many products such as chewing gum, tobacco, weapons, controlled drugs, obscene material, and other products considered to be obscene or dangerous. It is an offense if you are caught attempting to bring such products into the country. All luggage, including shopping bags, are x-rayed at every port of entry so no one can get away with sneaking such products into the country.

It did not make any sense to go home, so I stayed at my office to look into the matter and take the necessary actions. I called the Singapore police station and asked for the Singapore policeman by the name of Yuseff, whom the U.S. Marine Embassy Guard said was the point of contact. Fortunately for me, Yuseff was at the police station at the time I called. I identified myself as the U.S. Embassy Duty Officer and informed him that I was calling about the young American man who was arrested. We talked for about ten minutes on the procedures that would have to be followed that night. He said the judge would have to make a decision on whether to release the man to the U.S. Embassy or give him some jail time. Yuseff said jail time could be anywhere from one week to one month and possibly

## The Forgotten American

one year.

After getting the facts of the Singapore process for such violations, all I could do was ask that the young man be provided food for the evening and a bed to sleep in. Yuseff assured me that the young man would be given a bed and food for the evening. He also assured me the food was reasonably good and the bed and linens were clean. He then asked me to call him around 10:00 P.M. to see if the judge was available to discuss the matter. I requested that the young man be released to the embassy, that we would make sure he never committed such an obscene act again. He said he would relay that information to the judge when he arrived. The U.S. Embassy and the Singapore police department had a very good relationship, so it was rather easy to communicate with Yuseff.

After a couple of calls to the police station, I was told that the judge had an emergency and would not be coming to the police station until the morning. I inquired about the young American man who had been arrested earlier. I was told he received a clean bed and linens, including a blanket to keep warm. I was also informed that he ate some of the jail food and was now sleeping. After going over the Singapore criminal process again, Yuseff said he would call me in the morning at the embassy around 7:30 A.M.

The next morning, when I arrived at the embassy, my administrative assistant informed me that one of the Singapore policemen wanted me to call him as soon as I arrived. I asked if it was Yuseff, but she said it was a different policeman. When I called, the policeman informed me that the judge had requested that the young American man be released as soon as I called. He said the judge came to the police station around 6:00 A.M. and decided to release him to the embassy duty officer.

I was very relieved that the judge decided to turn the young American man to us. I thanked the policeman for the assistance I received from the Singapore police department.

Before I could ask to speak to the young American, the policeman said the American man wanted to speak to me before he left the police station. The police thanked me for staying in touch with the police department and then handed the phone to the American man. I introduced myself and asked him a series of questions, such as, "Were you briefed on the laws of Singapore and surrounding areas before you left the U.S.? If not, did the company you work for provide reading material on the laws that you must obey while doing business in Singapore? If reading material was provided, did you read the material to become familiar with the law and customs?" He answered yes to all my questions but admitted that he did not read the material very carefully. He also said he was eternally grateful that I was able to help him get released from jail. I told him I was glad he was released since there was a strong possibility of him spending anywhere from one week to a year in jail.

I decided it was not necessary to meet with him since he had already gone through enough drastic and frightening events. But I did tell him that if he ever attempted such a thing again while I was on call as the embassy duty officer, I would not come to his aid. I said I would let the Singapore judicial system impose whatever penalty they believed to be appropriate, which most likely would be jail time. He said he understood and promised never to do such a foolish thing again. I only hoped that he would never break any laws again while traveling throughout the world.

## Chapter 46

The transition of the acquisition support functions from Singapore to the Regional Procurement Support Office in Frankfurt, Germany, was accomplished without any political fights or problems. The only big task left for me to do was to find a home for the section of my office that provided acquisition support services to the U.S. Embassy in Singapore. After several discussions with the deputy chief of mission and the embassy administrative officer, it was decided to put my office and staff under the General Services Office. I spent the last six months preparing for the transfer of my office to that within the embassy. My staff would now be under the supervision of the director of the General Services Office but would retain their job titles and responsibilities. I sent several of my staff to training in Beijing and Hong Kong so that they could serve as team leaders upon my departure. The director of the General Services Office was very happy to know that my senior staff members would be able to help him in running the office.

One week before I was to depart Singapore for good, I sent a cable to all U.S. embassies and consulate generals in the two regions, reminding them that the RPSO in Singapore was to officially close at the end of August. On my last day, I sent another email message reminding everyone the RPSO was now officially closed and if assistance was needed, they should contact the U.S. Consulate General in Frankfurt, Germany.

My daughter, Casey, met me in Singapore on my last day. I had planned and scheduled a two-week vacation to China before returning to the U.S. We flew to Hong Kong and did some touring, visiting such places as Macau, Kowloon, and various islands around Hong Kong for several days. From there, we flew to Beijing and spent several days touring the countryside and climbing the Great Wall, which was easy for us since we are both marathon runners. We then flew back to Hong Kong with plans to do some touring in Shenzhen City in the Guangdong province of China, a border city south of Hong Kong. This trip did not pan out due to my big error of the week.

The day after we flew back from Hong Kong, we took the subway to customs at the border of Hong Kong, where we filled out applications to enter Guangdong province in China. We both returned our customs applications to the front desk at the same time. Casey was given a day pass very quickly, but the front desk took over thirty minutes to get back to me. When I was called to the customs desk, I was told I could not enter the Guangdong province because of my diplomatic passport. While rushing around to catch the train that morning, I had accidently picked up my diplomatic passport instead of my tourist passport.

I was informed that the passport to enter the province of Guangdong, China, was strictly for foreign tourists and for local people who wanted to tour and shop in the city of Shenzhen. My diplomatic passport obviously was seen as being on official diplomatic business. Since there were no U.S. embassies in the province of Guangdong, customs could not let me enter the province. Diplomatic passports can only be used for people who are on official business, so when diplomats want to travel as tourists, they need a regular passport.

Casey got her money back for the trip to Shenzhen, and we took the train back to Hong Kong. We ended up going to Causeway Bay, which is Hong Kong's major shopping district. We had the most wonderful time shopping and indulging in all types of Chinese food all afternoon. The next morning, Casey and I left for the United States. We flew from Hong Kong to the International Airport in Narita, Japan, where we caught the connecting flight to Los Angeles on Northwest Airlines. This flight was to arrive at the Los Angeles International Airport at 9:05 A.M. the next morning. This was supposed to give us enough time to connect to a nonstop flight on United Airlines to Washington Dulles Airport for arrival at 6:23 P.M. However, our flight from Japan was very late, and we missed our United Airlines flight. We also lost our business class seats, and we were very disappointed and angry as well.

The next morning, on September 8, 2001, Casey drove me to the Toyota dealership in Arlington, Virginia, to pick up my new Toyota. Two years prior to leaving for Singapore, I had purchased a new car from this same company. I had to sell that car back to them since I was not allowed to import my own car to Singapore. I purchased the new Toyota through the use of the Internet one month before I left Singapore. The manager at the dealership had promised to have my car ready on September 8, 2001, which was the date I gave him for me taking care of the paperwork and payment of the car. The manager, indeed, had the car polished and ready as well as the paperwork to be completed. After getting my car, I drove back to my home in Loudoun County, which was being painted. The rental agreement for my home had a provision that called for my current renters to move out one week before I returned to the U.S., so the house was now empty. Although the renters attempted to take care of the home, which was only two years old when I left the U.S., it now needed some minor repairs. After inspecting my home, I went to a nearby mini-mall, which had several hotels. I got a hotel for the week so I could check on the painting and minor repair to be done on my home. Casey, who lived about twenty miles from me, was not too pleased that I chose to stay in a hotel during that week. I explained to her that I wanted to be closer to home so that I could check on the painting and repair work at least once a day. I also told her I did not want to fight traffic from her home to my home every day. Twenty miles is not considered far, but traffic between my home and hers is horrendous.

The next two days were days of rest for me, which Casey found to be unusual. She had always known me to be busy around the clock and would tell me from time to time that "it is not normal." Once in a while, I would tell her that "not normal" is when people are lazy who sleep their lives away. Not only was I tired from the long flight home but from the many long hours of hard work abroad. I was so happy to be home in what I thought was a very safe country that was once owned by my ancestors.

## Chapter 47

After eating breakfast on September 11, 2001, I drove to my home to meet with a repairman who wanted to show me two types of front door panels that he wanted to install. After meeting with him, I did some errands before going back to the hotel. When I entered my hotel room, my telephone was ringing. I picked up the phone, and Casey asked me if I had the television on, and I said I just got home. She told me to turn it on and that one of the Twin Towers at the World Trade Center in New York City was burning. When I turned the television on, the tower was crumbling and, within seconds, there was smoke coming out of the second tower. Casey and I were not sure what was happening until ten minutes later, when one of the television stations announced that a plane had hit the World Trade building. Shortly thereafter, we found out there was an attack by foreign terrorists.

Both towers were now burning. I stood there watching the horror unfold before me. I was still standing as if frozen to the ground when one of the towers collapsed. My heart sank and I felt my body go weak so I sat down. I began to think of all the people inside the building and wondered if they could be saved. After seeing the second tower collapse, I became both sad and angry. My country had been attacked, and there was nothing I could do about it.

Later that morning, I found out that two other planes were hijacked. Four terrorists hijacked United Airlines 93 going from Newark, New Jersey, to San Francisco. All forty passengers, including the crew and the four hijackers, were killed. The second plane, American Airlines Flight 77, crashed into the Pentagon, killing 189 people.

I had come home to my country that I considered to be safe from hostile and evil enemies. A country that once belonged to my ancestors was under attack. A beautiful country that we Native Americans will never turn against, no matter how bad our ancestors were treated in colonial times and, to some extent, even in the twentieth century. I am probably one of the very few Native Americans who believe we are allowing too many people from foreign countries to become citizens. The U.S. opens its arms too readily when people cry "political asylum," and we let them enter our country. Does anyone think it is possible for some of these people to turn against us once they enter our country or that they have long-range plans to destroy America?

Both Casey and I went to college with many students from foreign countries. Guess what? Because we are Native Americans and not of the Caucasian race, some were so bold as to make disparaging remarks about our country and white America. Neither one of us stood by and listened to such garbage. Our response to such remarks was often harsh with blistering words in defending our country.

One of my biggest pet peeves is to see immigrants who have received U.S. citizenship flying flags from the country from which they immigrated. I often wonder if they still have full allegiance to that county. I also wonder if they miss their homeland and wish they could return. Sometimes I get angry and think it would be in their best interest to return to their original homeland. But I know I must keep an open mind and a compassionate heart. However, I firmly believe that people who seek U.S. citizenship should have total allegiance once they become full-fledged citizens of our country.

Immediately after the terrorist attacks of September 11, 2001, there were rumors that both men and women in certain parts of the U.S. were intimidating people on the streets who wore turbans or who looked like they were from the Middle East. I have no idea how they could determine who was from the Middle East. I also could not understand why these people thought anyone who looked Middle Eastern was a terrorist. But that was not too surprising to me; growing up in the Southwest, racism was rampant.

## Chapter 48

Two weeks after returning from abroad, I reported to my new position as Chief of Small Purchases, which I neither applied for nor requested. Prior to leaving my post abroad, I had notified my new director in Washington that I preferred a different position. She said they reorganized the department, which was now being implemented, and that there was no one who was qualified to hold that position. Upon my return to Washington, I found out this was not true. The woman who had held that position for many years was taken out of that position under the reorganization plan. She came to my office one day and told me they reassigned her to work with the White House. Her job sounded so interesting since she got to travel all over the world. I desperately wanted her job and told her so. She, however, said it was more like a clerical job and not at all glamorous or interesting.

There were crises every day in my new position, but it was not as demanding as my previous job. There was always a problem or two to solve with the delivery system to our embassies and consulate generals abroad. Despite these problems, I was able to go home after eight or nine hours of work. I had a long commute to my home, and traffic was often heavy and slow on the way home. While many commuters hated their long-distance commutes, I enjoyed them because I was able to solve many of the daily problems. It was also a "winding down" period for me.

A month after I started my new position in Washington, my manager called me to his office. He informed me that the Office of Foreign Missions (OFM) was searching for a new director for three of its programs. The OFM is responsible for providing benefits and services to the foreign diplomatic community residing in the U.S. The range of services provided includes the issuance of vehicle titles, registrations, driver's licenses, and license plates, processing tax exemption and duty-free customs requests; and facilitating acquisitions of property within local zoning law restrictions. My manager informed me that if I accepted the job, I would serve as the director for three programs: administration, finance, and federal acquisition. He said they wanted this person within one month and asked if I was interested. I said, "I am very much interested but will need to talk to the managing director of that office before I make a commitment."

Two weeks later, I was asked to meet with the managing director of the OFM. I was informed that the contractor support staff that worked on the premises desperately needed some guidance on the mission and policies of the office. I was further informed that the six field offices, located in San Francisco, Los Angeles, Houston, Miami, and New York City, were in dire need of assistance on agency policies and federal acquisitions rules and regulations. The information on the organization I received that day did not sound like it was another clean-up job, but I wanted to think about it for a week before I made a decision. I was hesitant in taking the job but decided to accept the position on the last day of the week that I promised to make a decision. My commute became even longer since the OFM was near the border of the state of Maryland and I lived in Virginia. The minute I stepped into my office at the OFM, I took off running with my new responsibilities. Lo and behold, it turns out that I was hired for another clean-up job. I was extremely disappointed, angry, and depressed all at the same time. I could see the word "sucker" written on my back. Nonetheless, I rolled up my sleeves and went to work. The first thing that needed attention was a new contract the office had offered to a small business company located in Alaska. I found a letter to OFM on my desk in which the company had requested several months for what it called "a consideration period." I was fit to be tied and immediately called them and reminded them that since they agreed to the contract prior to the formal offer, I needed an acceptance or rejection of the contract at the close of business. I also threatened to cancel the offer for a contract with them if I did not receive a response by the end of the day. Surprisingly, they responded within the hour of my telephone call and accepted the offer to do business with OFM.

Working around the clock with the federal acquisition specialist, I awarded the contract within two weeks. That was the beginning of a nightmare from which I did not wake up until one year later. After I awarded the contract, a consultant to the organization and a former diplomat came to my office. He thanked me for accepting the job and said the organization needed someone like me to clean the mess up. He went on to say they purposely looked for a woman director because they knew women were not only hard workers but had great multitasking skills. I was glad this very nice man was honest to tell me the truth, but the news was like a slap in the face. I was shocked and angry at the same time but tried not to show it.

I worked my butt off for the next year, cleaning up and streamlining the three programs. Funds were being spent like water, which I had to put under control since we were running out of funds. My staff and I worked tirelessly on updating and streamlining the organization's accounting system, updating old but useful policies and writing a few new ones, and administering two new support contracts in accordance with the appropriate terms and conditions. The most difficult task for me was in getting the contractors' support staff to work according to their contracts. The employees had grown accustomed to coming to work outside the normal federal working hours. Working with the program managers of the two contracts and government directors, unproductive employees were terminated and the productive ones were given training to improve their performance. Within a year, the organization was once again functioning well and within budget.

After one and one half years of hard work, I decided it was time to think about retiring from the federal government. I slowly started planning and preparing to retire at the end of my two years with the OFM. Being an energetic person and not yet ready to sit in my rocking chair, I started planning on working in the private sector. After completing and submitting my retirement papers, I registered for a month-long retirement seminar. The seminar was to help us plan for the next stage of our lives and the best way to replace the benefits that we derived from work. I had always understood that adjusting to life after retirement required a lot of planning. It is important to figure out how much money you will need to fund your desired lifestyle and how to spend your free time. I knew retirement would be a shock to my system if I did not plan on how to spend my free time in retirement. I thoroughly enjoyed my month-long seminar, which encompassed a multitude of issues associated with the retirement transition. This was the best seminar I ever attended in my entire life. I encourage all women in the workforce who are ready to retire to attend some type of retirement session. The session does not have to be a lengthy one; it can be a one-day or a week.

For the next month after retirement, I attended to many personal chores at home that I had put off for some time. I had my attorney update my living trust will and made sure that the few credit cards I had were all paid in full. I also paid a large amount of money toward the principal of my home mortgage, which left me with a very small balance. My plan was to pay off my mortgage within one year before moving to a new location. I wanted to pay for my next home in full so that I would not be bothered with mortgage payments. Some say that it is good to have a mortgage on your home, but I firmly believe if you can afford it you should pay for your home in full prior to retirement or when you retire. I do not recommend that young homeowners pay for their homes in full even if they can afford to do so. If you have extra money to spare, you should put it in a retirement account with your bank or other stable and well-known financial institutions.

Three weeks after I retired, I started sending out my resume to various companies that needed consultants to help them better understand the complexities of the federal acquisition process. Within two weeks, I accepted a job with a company close to home. I was back at work within one month after retirement. I was excited and felt like a young graduate student again. Upon informing my daughter, Casey, that I was going back to work in my field as a consultant in the private sector, she was shocked and annoyed. The first thing she said was, "Do you know how many people would like to retire today but cannot?" She went on to say that I should relax, read, travel, and do some limited volunteer work. I told her I enjoyed working and I was excited about working as a consultant in the private sector. She was more accepting of my new venture after I told her that my job was close to home and that I would be working only eight hours a day in accordance with my contract.

I really enjoyed working as a consultant in the private sector. I never knew that working only eight hours a day would be so wonderful. For the first time in many years, I began to relax and was able to slow down my fast pace work habits both at the office and home.

I was into my fourth year of consulting work when I ran into an acquaintance at a reception. We both had worked for the federal government for many years, and we were both now working as consultants. He recommended that I write a book on the federal acquisition process. He said the book would help young people who were entering the field of federal acquisitions. My acquaintance firmly believes in giving back to the community. He thought that by writing this book, I would be accomplishing this. He gave me the business card of the publishing company and encouraged me to submit a proposal to them.

Several weeks later, I did some searching on the publishing and training company located in Northern, Virginia. I decided right there and then to quit my consulting work and to write a book on federal acquisitions. I submitted a proposal and received a response a day later, requesting that I expand on the purpose of my book. Within a week, my proposal was accepted, and I was asked to sign a contract with the company. My contract gave me one year to complete the book. So I resigned from my position two months later and started writing. The book, titled *Federal Acquisition: Key Issues and Guidance,* was published in December 2009. I was very pleased overall with the way it turned out, moreover that I was encouraged by a former colleague to write it in the first place. The book has received several five-star ratings and is currently selling very well.

## Chapter 49

Suze Orman, the great financial advisor, a woman whom I admire and for whom I have great respect, says the following words at the end of her advisory sessions: "People first, then money, then things." My last words to you when facing marital discourse because of adultery are: "Children first, then money, then revenge when and if necessary." The welfare of the children, if any, must be the highest priority and not your revenge against the spouse who did you wrong. Yes, it definitely is worth your time to seek adequate child support. However, it is not worth your time and effort to seek money beyond child support unless your spouse is a millionaire or billionaire.

I am against women serving as "breadwinners" while their spouses are attending institutions of higher learning on a fulltime basis. Women too often have a need to help and nurture others before they help themselves. They need to start taking care of themselves first. In this day and age, it is very important for women to help themselves before helping their spouses attain an education. Why? Because the love and commitment made to them could be dissolved in the blink of an eye one day. It happened to me and other women. I could have been in a better financial position if I had put my wellbeing at the forefront during the ten years I tried to keep my family together.

It is important for women to work even if the family can live on one income. A workingwoman can support herself and her family if she gets divorced, is widowed, or if her husband loses his job. I encourage women to work because it will give them power and emotional rewards. Work can be to earn a paycheck or it can be volunteer work. I believe very strongly that life outside the home is healthy for women. They can gain personal fulfillment, and it helps them maintain their individual identities.

The pain and sorrow that one goes through when discovering your spouse is cheating or has cheated on you are beyond words and cannot be described definitely. When something like this happens to you, never look back or apologize for the action you took. And there is no such thing as closure, even though you may think there will be closure after the relationship ends. Yes, you will heal from the terrible blows of adultery, which in most cases lead to divorce, but there is never any real closure. The bad memories will pop up every once in a while, but they will not be so painful and will sometimes be replaced with anger. However, I will tell you one positive thing: THERE IS A BETTER TOMORROW regardless of the pain, sorrow, and suffering you go through during a difficult marriage and divorce. You can realize that better tomorrow through hard work and the determination and desire to beat all obstacles that lay in your path. And never forget to put the welfare of your children first and do what is best for them. That should be the highest priority in your decision-making process.